Praise for
JESUS, BREAD, AND CHOCOLATE

John Thompson has listened to the parable of his life and retold it in terms of coffee, chocolate, bread, and beer. What could be more deliciously compelling? It is only in community, gathered around a table laid with God's flavorful fare, that we learn to listen to and appreciate our lives. John has taught us just how this can be done.

MICHAEL CARD, songwriter, author, recording artist

———◆———

John Thompson lays out a wholesome and satisfying spread in this book, drawing together all sorts of rich and appealing ingredients: thoughtful biblical reflection; scenes from a difficult childhood; his experiences as a musician, pastor, and journalist; and a series of meditations on the making and enjoying of food. From beginning to end, John whets our appetite for something more filling—and more life-giving—than processed food or processed faith.

STEVE GUTHRIE, PhD, associate professor of theology at Belmont University

———◆———

For a generation, John J. Thompson has been deep in the skunkworks experimenting, helping to create and ultimately inhabiting an expression of the Christian faith that is sorely needed today. His new book offers a helpful vision grounded in theology and informed by real-life practitioners. What once was an outsider, "alternative" lifestyle now offers a life-giving balm to the American church.

NICK PURDY, founder of Wild Heaven Craft Beers and *Paste* magazine

John Thompson's new book fosters not only a renaissance of good taste but a concomitant hunger for real spirituality that is an inextricable part of real humanness.

TOM WILLETT, music industry consultant and author, www.tomwillett.com

This book is important. It captures an idea that is contagious and living. There's a problem in our culture at large, the cause of which has never really been exposed—in my mind—until now. John Thompson puts his finger on it. *Jesus, Bread, and Chocolate* is more than just a study of the artisan crafts of bread making, coffee roasting, and beer brewing. It's almost an indictment of the Industrial Revolution ... *Almost*, because it's not really the Industrial Revolution that is to blame, of course. It is each of us. The machinery only accelerated our shallow and sinful tendency to ruin things. But Thompson's isn't a radical cry to destroy the automation and assembly lines of industrialism; it is simply a call to be mindful of how we live; to extract the precious from the worthless. His stories fit together seamlessly, build on one another, and collectively pack a big punch. They trace the problem in small, personal, specific areas and, without straining, reveal how the dislocation from our true identity leaves us yearning for a reconnect. He then lovingly points to a resolution that's within our reach.

DOUG VAN PELT, founder of *HM Magazine*

In *Jesus, Bread and Chocolate*, John J. Thompson serves up a delectable mix of personal story, keen observations of evangelical culture, and scriptural reflection. The result is a filling and satisfying meal for the growing number of people in our churches who are starving for something more substantial than consumer Christianity.

C. CHRISTOPHER SMITH, coauthor of *Slow Church* and editor of *The Englewood Review of Books*

What should Christians do about theologies and practices that have lost their flavor in a culture of commodification and consumption? John Thompson examines the growing renaissance in handcrafted, artisanal approaches to making bread, coffee, chocolate, beer, and music and finds engaging metaphors for spiritual discovery and renewal. *Jesus, Bread, and Chocolate* is shot through with the spirit of the times and shows Thompson as what he has long been—a tastemaker.

DAVE PERKINS, MDiv, PhD, associate director of the Religion in the Arts and Contemporary Culture program at The Divinity School at Vanderbilt University

———◆———

A breezy journey into the quest for faith that is holistic, organic, and deindustrialized.

SHAWN DAVID YOUNG, PhD, assistant professor of music at York College of Pennsylvania and author of *Gray Sabbath*

———◆———

Humanity searches for truth in almost every aspect of life. *Jesus, Bread, and Chocolate* not only encourages us to continue our search; it explains that there are, in fact, answers if we continue to seek. In my own life, I have desperately wanted to encounter God. After reading this book, I see that I do experience his hand. I was looking for him in the earthquake and in the fire, but the Lord wasn't in the earthquake or in the fire; he is in the gentle whisper of our daily routines, the coffee we share with a friend in need, or even the passion and dreams we discuss with a family member over a local stout. The topics in the book are both timely and eternal, and John's writings have encouraged me to craft my story with greater purpose and intention.

STEPHEN CHRISTIAN, songwriter and vocalist of Anberlin

Jesus, Bread, and Chocolate is fresh and enlightening. I plan on keeping it close by, especially as I travel. This book helps me feel close to the family, friends, and wonderful community of musicians here in Nashville whom I so love. John's stories and his memories of discovering and rediscovering music and the power of the arts remind me that it is all spiritual as it weaves itself into the fabric of our lives. John is an intelligent man with lots of talent and heart. He writes from a different perspective that encourages me to keep doing what I've been gifted and called to do. I see why the psalmist implores us to "taste and see that the Lord is good." I pray we can all be an enticing aroma to others for the One who valued a good meal and beverage with his friends.

PHIL KEAGGY, songwriter, recording artist, guitarist

———◆———

What do bread, coffee, chocolate, beer, and "twangy" music have to do with Jesus? It turns out, quite a lot. In *Jesus, Bread, and Chocolate*, John Thompson melds memoir and experimentation, showing us how the basic stuff of life like food and music turn out not to be so basic after all, but instead are an avenue for renewed connection, joy, and faith. This book isn't just about "hipster" values; it's about grounding those of us who have felt disconnected from authenticity—and not just from where our coffee or tomatoes come from, but from the gospel. The good stuff takes more time; it costs us more. It's also messy and full of what Thompson calls "twang." *Jesus, Bread, and Chocolate* is about learning how to cultivate our tastes again for food and faith that connect us with flavor and mystery. Thompson helps us see that embracing authenticity in all areas of our lives, from food to relationships, brings us closer to who we want to be and what we suspected Christianity was really about. This book is satisfying, but I must warn you: it will make you hungry … for the good stuff.

AMY HUGHES, PhD, assistant professor of theology at Gordon College

John J. Thompson has always been a compass for finding the True North of good music. Now he's doing that for the yearnings of the human heart. John speaks to our need for something real, something with roots. There's a whole world of prepackaged, artificial, unwholesome faith out there. John points us to something different.

JOEL J. MILLER, blogger (*Two Cities*) and author of *Lifted by Angels*

———◆———

John Thompson is a man who knows real music. He just has that "sense" thing happening—and he has no problem telling you what he sees through his lens. Like he says, he'll do his best to ruin you for "the cheap stuff." *Jesus, Bread, and Chocolate* is easy to read and leaves you pondering some things you may not have considered from the rut you might be in. One thing is certain: if you let John be a guide, you know when you are indulging in the "real thing."

JERRY BRYANT, Full Circle Media Group

———◆———

It was sometime in the 1980s or early '90s, hot as blazes outside, in the middle of Cornerstone Festival. I was debating a young John Thompson on feminism—me the liberal to his gently conservative position. (If the topic had been drinking alcohol, we'd have changed places.) But the conversation took a turn into personal bios, and I sensed in him a deeply kindred spirit. He dared to share things about his terrifying childhood and journey toward God—things only a transparently humble and self-reflective person could dare. His story "twanged" something deep within me, an echoing string played by the same invisible fingers. The book you hold is from a man no longer as young in years but still majoring in the ability to tell the truth in love ... and with a twang (more on the latter in his book!). I hope you read it with an eye to discovering something real that first captures one's attention and then captures one's heart, soul, and life.

Jon Trott, former editor of *Cornerstone* magazine and coauthor of *Selling Satan*

———◆———

Essential items are mere commodities in our mass-market culture, and we often miss out on the vitality and art that consumerism trades in for ease and comfort. This neutering of the nutrients isn't just confined to the food industry, but as John Thompson points out, it is affecting our lives of faith. While looking into the worlds of handcrafted bread, chocolate, beer, music, and more, Thompson helps us realize that our relationship with God may be "enriched" with nonvital elements that take away the satisfaction we yearn for. If you want a primer of the inner workings of an organic faith that is impacted by artisans and practitioners from other walks of handcrafted life, I doubt you'll find a better book than *Jesus, Bread, and Chocolate.*

RANDY ROSS, blogger and marketing specialist for The Parable Group

JESUS,
BREAD, *and*

Crafting a HANDMADE FAITH
IN A MASS-MARKET WORLD

CHOCOLATE

JOHN J. THOMPSON

ZONDERVAN®

ZONDERVAN

Jesus, Bread, and Chocolate
Copyright © 2014 by John Joseph Thompson

This title is also available as a Zondervan ebook. Visit www.zondervan.com/ebooks.

Requests for information should be addressed to:
Zondervan, *3900 Sparks Dr. SE, Grand Rapids, Michigan 49546*

Library of Congress Cataloging-in-Publication Data

Thompson, John.
    Jesus, bread, and chocolate : crafting a handmade faith in a mass-market
    world / John Thompson.
        p. cm.
        ISBN 978-0-310-33939-7 (softcover)
    1. Subject one. 2. Subject two. I. Title.
    AA000.0.A00 2015
    000.00—dc23   2014000000

Cover design: Brian Bobel, Dual Identity, Inc.
Chapter title page photography: See page 265
Interior design: Denise Froehlich

First Printing February 2015 / Printed in the United States of America

To my grandparents, Nicki and Gerald Gordon Holton,
for the legacy of love, faithfulness, grace, hospitality, and integrity
you have established for our family,
and to my wife, Michelle, and my amazing children,
Jordan Joseph, Wesley James, Trinity Michelle, and Jesse Gordon.
I can't wait to see all that you craft
with the gifts God has given you.

CONTENTS

NEW RESPECT FOR THE TWANG

ou know, John," my friend Buddy said over breakfast at Grandma Sally's Pancake House, "I would suggest that maybe it's not the twang you don't like about modern country music, but the absence of twang."

It was 1995. Buddy Miller had played a show at my concert venue in Wheaton, Illinois, the night before with his wife, Julie, and a singer-songwriter named Randy Stonehill, who was a bit of a legend in my little world. I had known Buddy casually for a few years and loved the way he and Julie played together. My wife and I had them on a bit of a pedestal, in fact. Their brutally honest, transparent, unadorned style emboldened us in our own musical pursuits. I jumped at the chance to have breakfast with Buddy.

As we ate, Buddy asked me about our music and our influences. I rambled on about my eclectic tastes—from Johnny Cash and Bob Dylan to gospel music like the Fairfield Four and Blind Boys of Alabama to modern rock like U2. I also mentioned that my wife, Michelle, and I had found some musical common ground in the sounds of artists like Merle

Haggard, Patsy Cline, Emmylou Harris, Maria McKee, and the Eagles. "I love old country," I insisted. "I just don't like the twangy stuff like Garth Brooks and Shania Twain."

Buddy proceeded to school my sorry twenty-four-year-old self with great patience and grace. "The twang is the essence of American music," he said. "It's in the high, lonesome sound of bluegrass. It's in the field hollers and angst of gospel. It's in the tension and release of the blues and the bent strings of rock and roll." He went on to tell of how Nashville producers removed the authentic twang from country music and replaced it with strings and lush production to make it more palatable to mainstream audiences. They then added some pseudo-twang back in as a kind of musical window dressing. It sounded fake. Unsatisfying.

"That stuff you say you like," Buddy said respectfully, "is full of twang. Heck, Bob Dylan is practically nothing *but* twang."

I felt—I'm not kidding here—like a light was shining on our little corner booth, and God in heaven was saying, *Pay attention, John. This is important!* I did pay attention, and my heart started to race. So many things began to make sense in that moment.

The music I craved, sought out, and spent my life talking about had always been laced with *twang*—whether it was country or metal or folk or gospel. Buddy had simply given me a new understanding of the word—a word I would have ignorantly run away from a few minutes earlier. Actually, he reappropriated a word I had used disdainfully and imbued it with new and exciting meaning.

By the time of my breakfast with Buddy, I was already
a music journalist and aspiring pop culture historian
covering a tiny niche of faith-fueled, mostly independent,
subtly spiritual alternative music. I invested in words like
authenticity and *integrity* as I circled the indescribable
essence of music that captivated me. I suppose by devoting
so much time to writing about music, I have, in fact, spent
my life "dancing about architecture," as Elvis Costello once
said in an interview. That may seem absurd, I suppose,
until a building really makes you want to cut a rug. When
I come across music or anything else that carries the aroma
of another, more real dimension than the one in which I'm
currently trapped, you will always see my toes start tapping.
I know I am not alone in this.

And it wasn't just music that charmed me with its twang.
I started hearing the twang everywhere — and noticing its
absence when it went missing. It can be felt in the tension
of a loving, vulnerable relationship. It can be tasted in good
food and drink. When the twang is removed from these
things, they go down easier but satisfy less. It's much easier
to maintain a shallow connection with someone than to
cultivate a real friendship. No one has to develop a taste for
sugary, salty, processed food, but it can take effort to learn
how to like *real* food.

Nowhere is this reality more important than in the
cultivation of our faith life. Millions of Americans are losing
their taste for processed, convenient, consumerist Christianity. We have gorged ourselves on cheap church for decades
and have become, as Randy Stonehill sang, "undernourished

and overfed." The gospel we are living has, in many cases, lost its saltiness. What good is it? We have created a Jesus made in our own image; a light-haired, blue-eyed, fair-skinned, corporate-friendly, feel-good American guru with absolutely no discernable twang.

I grew up a product of a highly automated and manufactured culture that prided itself on removing all of the rough edges and twang from my world. It felt as if the values of the Industrial Revolution found their full expression during my coming of age in the 1970s and '80s. I had no idea how much farther we had to fall. Cheaper, easier, faster, more—these are the tenets of our increasingly globalized neighborhood. I am hungry for something deeper, something truer, something chewy and challenging and risky. Although I didn't know it at the time Buddy and I sipped our coffee and talked about music, I was teetering on the edge of a personal, professional, and spiritual catastrophe I didn't see coming. I was going to need some twang to get me through. Thank God I found it.

I've run down many rabbit trails in my obsession with twang. You'll get a feel for that as you read these stories and listen in on my conversations with coffee gurus, bakers, chocolate makers, brewers, and others I've encountered along the way. I'm losing my taste for the prepackaged, the mass-produced, and the canned. It's no longer enough to add water, microwave, stir, and eat. I want to know where things come from. I want to know how they affect me. I want to know how they were supposed to taste before the factories took over. I search obsessively for the good, the true, and the beautiful in the grooves of an LP, the pages of a book, the frames of a film, and the conversations and prayers I share with a small group of fellow pilgrims in our home. In these pages I'm going to do my best to ruin you for the cheap stuff. Ultimately, it doesn't matter what kind of coffee you drink; it is the kind of faith you live, or the kind of faith you abandon, that can make all the difference in the world.

I've noticed that most human endeavors fit somewhere on a continuum between manufactured and handmade, between plastic and flesh. Millions of people are intentionally moving backward on that continuum, seeking out handmade things and communal experiences in ways that buck a couple of thousand years of one-way commercial "progress." I was recently looking up recipes on my iPhone while walking through a farmers market and simultaneously texting my wife about the shopping list she'd given me. The irony was not lost on me. I am a fan of technology, and I stand in awe of its potential for good or for ill on a minute-by-minute basis in my life. But the spiritual, social, ethical, and emotional conundrum facing all of us is much more complex than analog versus digital.

I'm following hints of this "crafted" approach to life and faith like they're breadcrumbs leading me deeper and deeper into an enchanted forest. It chills me to think of the toxic effect industrial fumes are having on our relationships, art and imagination, and even on how we understand and interact with the designer of all of this stuff. Too many people are giving up on Jesus because of the corporate accent of his people. Many find much more satisfying community at the local pub or coffee shop than at church. My artisanal spelunking, however, is showing me that we don't need to hand out suspenders and moustache grooming tools to our worship teams or replace all of the lights in our churches with Edison bulbs in order to correct the unfortunate pall industrialism has cast over the church. We just need to stop and smell the coffee.

Every real awakening is personal. This journey has been a very personal one, but as you will see, I am a continually evolving product of some peculiar and wonderful communities. While the stories and conversations contained in these pages are my own, the implications resonate far beyond my own walls. I'm a musician and a music industry professional. I'm a husband and a father. I'm a songwriter and a roaster and a brewer and a gatherer. In the ways that matter, I bet you are too. These stories may be mine in the literal sense, but my conversations over the last decade about the ideas and experiences covered here have shown that many of us are combing these same beaches for glimmers of a renewed vision. It's time for us to figure out what the surface stuff—the beards and the campaigns to buy local and the community gardens—tells us about where our own hearts and our neighbors' hearts really are.

Maybe bread and chocolate and coffee and farmers markets can show us something about what it means to cultivate a taste for real community, real humanity, and real discipleship. It may seem frivolous to some. It may feel threatening to purveyors of the status quo. But our ability to rediscover and embrace an authentic faith in the authentic Jesus may, in fact, be a matter of spiritual life or death.

Chapter 1

THE ROAD TO RUINATION

My biological father was a charming, articulate, sociopathic mess of a human being. His mother taught him how to get away with check fraud, and it's unclear if he ever did an honest day's work in his life. He was a controlling, abusive, alcoholic monster who could change, without a second's notice, into an exuberant, hilarious clown. If he had been more disciplined, he would have made a good mobster.

He was a con man by trade—or at least that's the best we can figure. He scammed people and then disappeared. His life was about hiding from the law while living large. He had a car phone in his fancy ride, while his wife and kids were scrimping by on welfare. His fraudulence sent me searching desperately for the truth at a very young age.

We moved a lot when I was young. For several months during the summer of '77, we were basically homeless. My brother and I stayed with my grandparents while my father and my pregnant mother drove around Illinois trying to find a new place to live. We eventually settled on a run-down farm outside of Peoria, Illinois, for a couple of years. It was the longest we ever lived in one place, so I used to say I grew up on that farm. The truth is that in many ways I was forced to grow up before we moved to the farm. I was seven then.

My mom became a Christian when I was about three years old. By that I mean she transformed from a well-mannered Episcopalian into a young woman who believed that Jesus was alive and real and available to her. A spiritual phenomenon that *LIFE* magazine referred to as "the Jesus Movement" inspired millions of young people to connect with Jesus in a very personal, intimate, and communal way. Once these Jesus people got to Mom, I was a quick convert. At three years old, I began developing my own relationship with God. My faith, in fact, predates my conscious memories.

My earliest church-related memories include the high, vaulted ceilings and haunting choral singing of the Episcopal and Catholic churches, and the joyful mayhem of Mom's early charismatic Bible study groups. It was a pretty normal occurrence to hear people speaking in tongues and to see them laying hands on people during prayer and searching large, leather-bound Bibles for answers. I remember when my mom got baptized. It was a strange thing to see these people I barely knew take her into a lake and dunk her under the water. She came out crying. I was upset. I ran to her — ready to protect her from these strange people — but she told me the tears were happy tears. Jesus was in her heart. I was used to seeing her cry, but this was different.

She stayed with my father for seven more years, until I was

not quite ten, because she did not believe that divorce was acceptable in God's eyes. Mom wore long sleeves to cover the bruises on her arms when she took us to the beach. At one point, things got bad enough that we moved to my grandparents' house in the Chicago suburbs. After a few months, my father managed to convince her he had changed. He had "found the Lord." He even became the pastor of a storefront church.

Yes, you read that correctly. He preached up a storm at that little church, cried like a televangelist on the evening news, and then went right back to the same old, same old once we moved back in with him. I hated him and feared him, and I was mystified by him and terrified of becoming him. I defined myself, to the best of my abilities, as his complete opposite.

Late one night, he came home drunk and armed with a large handgun. With me on his right knee, and my brother on his left, he waved his .38 just inches from my right ear as he threatened to kill my mother and take away my brothers and me if she ever tried to leave him. There were four of us boys by then, and though she believed divorce to be a sin, Mom rightly understood that leaving us to be raised by him would be a greater sin. It was time for us to flee.

Unfortunately, she had no idea how to escape. One day while she was at a community college in town, a couple of college students approached her tentatively. They explained that while they had never done anything like this before, as they had been praying, they felt strongly compelled by God to approach her to tell her she needed to escape some kind of situation, and they were going to do whatever they could to help facilitate that escape. These complete strangers coordinated the details with her, and within a few weeks, a pickup truck carried us and our belongings away while my father was in court.

Because of my father's criminal connections, we had to go into hiding. We lived at a rescue mission called Wayside Cross in Aurora, Illinois, for a while and then moved to a Christian summer camp for underprivileged and at-risk youth on the Fox River in St. Charles. We couldn't say good-bye to our friends. We couldn't call our grandparents. We had to completely disappear.

Months later, the police assured my mother that it was safe for us to come out of hiding. We moved back in with my grandparents in Lombard, a typical Chicago suburb. My parents divorced shortly thereafter, and somehow, our father was granted visitation of us boys every other weekend. We then experienced a season of psychological warfare, as he did everything in his power to use us to convince our mother to return to him. He read me Scriptures about divorce and wives submitting to husbands, and he wept juicy tears as he testified to his undying love for her and us. My youngest brother was just a baby and was already showing symptoms of post-traumatic stress disorder. Excessive acid in my stomach—in part the result of near constant stress—caused me to throw up every night. I was pale and skinny, and my eyes were dark. I was falling apart physically, psychologically, and spiritually.

On my thirteenth birthday, my father called, and I, at my counselor's suggestion, finally let him have it. I swore and cried and screamed at him. After our conversation, he told my mother that if she ever remarried, he would find her and kill her. My grandfather heard the whole thing on the other line and made sure my father knew it. My mom called the police and filed a report. My father disappeared.

My mom had met a man at our church. He was a relatively new Christian and had recently gone through a divorce himself. He and Mom clicked, and despite the incredible baggage involved, he married her and took us all on.

I had recurring nightmares about killing my father. I begged God to send his car off a bridge, then prayed for forgiveness for having such evil thoughts. My "personal relationship with Jesus" involved lots of screaming at the heavens, pounding my fists into the earth, and reading Romans 8:28: "And we know that in all things God works for the good of those who love him, who have been called according to his purpose." I read it over and over, trying to make sense of my life. That verse drove me crazy.

I tried to stop believing in God, but it never worked. There was just too much evidence all around me. Everywhere I looked, I saw his fingerprints. Music, art, nature, kisses, the sun and the moon—it all pointed to him. I believed in God, but I thought he had forgotten about us or was punishing us for our father's sins, like I gleaned from my reading of Exodus 20:5, where God is said to be "a jealous God, punishing the children for the sin of the parents to the third and fourth generation . . ."

As terrible as my biological father was, the rest of my family is incredible. I am blessed to have grown up with a loving, attentive, and extremely cool extended family and with mentors and heroes who celebrated my eccentricities and encouraged my headfirst approach to making sense of the world around me. When I kicked against what I perceived to be stale traditions, they were gracious and patient. When I asked what I was sure were deep questions, they honored me and gave me thoughtful answers. I see now that my instinct to handcraft my faith instead of settling for the off-the-shelf version that wasn't working for me was inspired, encouraged, and enabled by family members and close friends.

Life as I saw it unfolding spoke of humanity's fall and evil and the serpent and death and pain, but a deeper reality gripped my heart and has never let me go. The flame of faith could not be extinguished by abuse and terror. A few months after that terrible phone call on my thirteenth birthday, I made a conscious decision to begin to find a way to forgive my father so the pain and anger wouldn't consume me. At one point, I regularly attended five different youth groups. I was an aggressive seeker and was interested in the different ways various churches sought God's truth. As a teen, I read theological books I could barely understand by Francis Schaeffer, C. S. Lewis, and G. K. Chesterton because my mentors read those books. Mostly, though, I dug for truth in music and conversations.

I now realize that throughout my teen years I was sheltering in a grove of tall, nurturing trees. I often felt alone, or I liked to imagine myself as some kind of pioneer, but in hindsight

I see I was just a bucking lamb in a very safe corral. I remember regularly dressing as obnoxiously as possible for church, just to irritate "traditional" people. I wore fake leather pants, studded leather wristbands, and a ripped-up shirt, and I spiked up my hair as high as it would go. I scrawled Bible verses and lyrics from Christian songs on my jackets and jeans. I challenged every vestige of traditional church life I could find—always kicking against the pricks and deeply desperate for it all to be real. My grandparents, aunts, uncles, and parents' friends were eventually joined by priests, pastors, youth ministers, volunteer "big brothers," songwriters, and other role models—all doing their best to equip me to thrive.

It seemed clear to me from a young age that truly authentic people inhabited all types of spiritual environments. I remember profound and life-changing conversations with priests and Sunday school teachers at St. Mark's Episcopal Church and sermons delivered by nondenominational pastors that were easy to understand and apply to my life. As a teen, I found my place among a tribe of edgy rock-and-roll Christians deeply invested in issues of cultural relevance, social justice, and good, clean fun. In all of these varied environments, I have been profoundly blessed and lovingly tolerated.

Some of my heroes were people I actually knew, while others were musicians and songwriters I admired from a distance. Terry Scott Taylor sang acerbic, haunting faith songs in his tragically unknown band, Daniel Amos, while Greg Hill mentored me through confirmation and youth group. Obscure rock bands, filmmakers, authors, parish priests, extended family, and high school friends formed a spiritual and cultural tapestry that covered me like a cloak during some very confusing years. The gospel modeled for me was not one of fear or retreat; it was a careful balance of improvisation and faithfulness. I do not take these relationships and experiences for granted. They not only helped me survive but also tuned my heart to see and hear things differently.

Someone set up this world, filled it with all the necessary elements, started it spinning, and seems to enjoy interrupting its gradual and temporary decay with glimpses of a bright and glorious future. "The kingdom of heaven has come near," Jesus said. It's not far-off in the future. It's here, right now; yet it's still not yet. The brokenness in me, and in the world around me, is groaning to be repaired. There's a beat to it, a cadence. All creation points toward this someday coming and present healing. People with ears to hear can detect its patterns. I want to be a person who hears.

WELCOME TO THE SUBURBS

My life didn't begin to resemble anything normal until I was a teen in the Chicago suburbs. Having grown up "on the lam," I hadn't benefited from peer groups, social cues, or a common culture. Lots of kids don't fit in. I, however, was terrified of boys my age. I made up stories about myself because the truth was too hard to talk about.

Once, in sixth grade, when the kids in class were taking turns telling the group what their fathers did for a living, I froze. One kid's dad had been a Stormtrooper in Star Wars. Several other dads were doctors or engineers. When it was my turn, I panicked. But I'd seen a documentary on PBS about the history of Chicago's lakefront and how hundreds of men had basically built a big chunk of the city out over the water. "My dad dug Lake Michigan," I blurted out. The other kids laughed. The teacher laughed. I tried to moderate my lie. "Well, he didn't dig it by himself; he had lots of help." I was mortified. I had no idea what my father actually did. I just knew it was illegal and that I wasn't supposed to walk home alone because my mom and grandparents were afraid he would abduct me. But I couldn't say that. I never did.

From the time I was very young—maybe five or six—music was my escape from the pain and confusion of life. At one point in the late 1970s, probably around age eight, I was given a set of stereo radio receiver headphones that would have to be considered the primordial ancestors of the Sony Walkman that would debut a few years later. They were enormously bulky and had an antenna that stuck up from one side. Those goofy headphones and I were inseparable. They were like a secret door to another dimension. In order to keep them on my head when I rode my bike, I had to tighten them down with a bungee cord. I would sneak them on in bed and slowly dial through AM radio stations coming in from as far away as Chicago. Once we moved to the Chicago area, one of my favorite ways to spend a day was to ride my bike to the library and check out a dozen LPs (the limit)—everything from *Hotel California* to the *Star Wars* sound track to Mahler's Fifth Symphony. I would lie down on the floor listening to records, writing stories, painting pictures, or trying to play along on my guitar.

We attended a variety of churches until we settled in at my grandparents' Episcopal church. Once my biological father was out of the picture, my mom married Tom Thompson, the fascinating, goateed college man she had met at church. He began to unconditionally love my three younger brothers and me, though none of us were "normal." He'd played in rock bands during the 1960s, so he and I bonded over music. I needed a bit longer than my brothers to trust that he would stick around, but by the end of eighth grade, I took his name. When I was eighteen, he adopted me. To this day, I consider him one of my best friends. This father let me listen to his records, and he taught me how to play the guitar. Whenever I refer to "Dad," he's the one I'm talking about.

◆

Sociologically speaking, I am a member of Generation X. I'm the oldest son of a baby boomer. I came of age during the 1970s and '80s, awash in popular culture, emerging technology, and skyrocketing consumerism. The arbiters of cool neatly subdivided my generation into "markets," then sold us all the corresponding accessories. I fell into the "alternative" camp. I knew a few real people who were on the same wavelength, but most of my community was virtual. I stayed up late to watch *U2 Live at Red Rocks* on MTV, and I imagined that all those people in the rain were My People. I read magazines and imagined sitting at a table with writers and artists talking about stuff that really mattered, while the ignorant masses listened to dumb music and ate white bread. I watched movies and imagined the offbeat girl would notice me and appreciate me as a Curator of Interesting and Meaningful Ideas rather than see me as Awkward Teenage Dork.

When I discovered a somewhat underground world of Jesus-loving rock-and-roll artists, I was more than a little intrigued. One of the first records I found was by a hard rock group from a gritty neighborhood in Chicago. They were called Resurrection Band, and they blew my mind. They played seriously hard rock that was every bit as good, or better, than anything my friends were listening to. They also lived in an "intentional community" called Jesus People USA with hundreds of other radical Christians. They served the poor and the elderly. They worked hard and blessed the urban world around them. Talk about authenticity! I begged God to "call" me to move in with them. He never did.

Several members of JPUSA became friends, mentors, and cultivators of my growing understanding of the gospel message. They published a magazine called *Cornerstone*, which tackled the most difficult and controversial issues of the day. When I was thirteen, they started a music festival of the same name. I attended one day of that first Cornerstone Festival in Grayslake, Illinois, just a few days before my fourteenth birthday. An instant city had been crafted out of tents, barns, generators, and PA equipment, and I experienced a kind of community I hadn't even known I was craving. It was as if a glowing path had appeared in front of me. I'd found my tribe.

Cornerstone was about blowing past the comfortable edges of the modern evangelical experience and daring to take Jesus at his word. Sure, the music was far more engaging, culturally relevant, and diverse than any other Christian festival in the country, but it didn't stop there. The event offered dozens of thoughtful seminars led by brilliant people who tackled everything from sex and dating to cultivating a biblically sound theology of social justice. The music seminar focused on aspects of personal discipline and accountability that would allow artists to maintain their integrity in the midst of a world of compromise. The event included emotionally powerful worship, intellectually challenging teaching, opportunities to serve others, and mosh pits. The first time I raised my hands in worship was when the Orange County pop punk band Undercover played an amped-up version of the hymn "Holy, Holy, Holy." Cornerstone was a wonderfully euphoric and deeply pragmatic playground of faith, art, mind, and soul that gathered outsiders and insiders for a few days' worth of heaven on earth.

By the time I turned fifteen, I had a vision of how I would speak order into my own chaos. I would become a youth pastor or social worker (or both), one who wrote and performed my own music and helped introduce others my age to this underground world of faith-fueled rock and roll. I would have a record store, a concert venue, and maybe even a radio station—and it would be called True Tunes. I would incubate a culturally relevant community and turn people on to a fresh (and, I thought, new) understanding of who Jesus really is and what he's all about. It wouldn't be about the dirty word *religion*—at least not about my understanding of what religion was. It would be about a love that was so pure and so powerful it would pulse through broken, sinful people and bless the entire creation. And it wouldn't be some utopian hippie love either. This would be a love that cost something. It would be a love that made big claims and then lived up to them. It would be a love with teeth.

Chapter 2

THIS MEANS SOMETHING!

A new friend is sitting in my East Nashville living room, holding a cup of coffee he has been looking forward to for a while. He tastes it and smiles. "This is amazing," he says. Sure, he actually likes the coffee, but there's more to it than that. Much more. I can relate to Richard Dreyfuss's characterization of Roy Neary in *Close Encounters of the Third Kind*, who, when he contemplated a mound of mashed potatoes, exclaimed, "This means something! This is important!" This cup of coffee means something to me and to my friend—something important, something communal, spiritual, and true.

I had told my friend earlier about how I roast my own coffee—which sounds much more involved and exotic than it actually is. Knowing he was coming over, I had roasted some coffee beans. When he arrived, I ground the beans and brewed a cup for him. I told him the beans came from Papua, New Guinea, and two of my other guests perked right up. Their sister, it turns out, was on a long-term mission trip to this remote island. They both eagerly asked if they could have a cup. I'm not even sure they like coffee in general, but they definitely liked *this* coffee.

These beans come from the Nebilyer Valley in New Guinea, an area that functioned primarily as a battlefield between warring tribes and clans until an explorer arrived in the 1930s. The tribes, seemingly weary of the nonstop violence, invited this man to build his home right in the middle of the battlefield so he could help mediate conflicts between them. He introduced them to the cultivation of coffee and established the necessary infrastructure to support the new endeavor. The warring ended, and cultivation began. Eighty years later, the harmony and artistry are still going strong. A small-scale broker works with the folks in New Guinea and sends the green coffee beans to my supplier in Wisconsin. I buy them online, roast them, grind them, and brew my coffee. It not only makes me feel good to be supporting something that literally brings peace where there once was war, but it makes me look really cool to serve coffee this good. As spiritually minded as I want you to believe I am, I also desperately want you to think I'm cool.

I love serving guests a cup of my coffee — or, when appropriate, a home-brewed beer. My wife has a collection of teacups from all over the world — each with a unique story. She loves few things as much as having a relaxing cup of tea with a friend. Michelle and I are wired to welcome people and to make them feel at home. It's actually the main reason we moved to Nashville. Life is about people, and we increasingly have little time for anything that fails to bring us closer to the people God places in our life.

WATER FROM A DEEPER WELL

"I'm a big fan of Jesus," a young woman tells me at a Foo Fighters concert during the South by Southwest festival in Austin, Texas, "but I could never call myself a Christian." I had been pushed into close contact with this woman and another person I incorrectly assumed was her friend, by the massive crowd that surrounded us. She mentioned being seriously hurt by religion, and though I wasn't yet officially a part of their discussion, I couldn't help but react with a look of chagrin. She noticed the expression on my face and immediately pulled me, a complete stranger, into the conversation.

I told her I was pretty sure Jesus was heartbroken by many of the things done in his name, and that I was sure I had been a party to that heartbreak in my own life, and that I was sure glad he came with a message of forgiveness and grace. "Yeah," she said, "it's hard to know what to think about what he said and did when the people who taught you about him were so full of hate, hypocrisy, and anger."

A half hour of eager conversation followed, as we discussed whether or not truth was knowable, what Jesus' claims and purposes actually were, and how critical it should be for any spiritually minded person to dig through the cultural and religious muck to find the treasure on offer from him — all at a rock concert at Stubb's BBQ. In the background, John Fogerty, who had joined the Foos that night, sang "Fortunate Son."

It's more and more common to hear experts talk about how the church in America is dying. Young adults are increasingly identifying as "religiously unaffiliated" in the global West, and churches are closing their doors in record numbers. For some, it's the perceived confluence of Christianity and politics that turns them off; for others, it's the shock any claim of exclusivity or absolute truth causes in a pluralistic, postmodern culture. Many fail to ever even hear Jesus through the noise of a pseudo-Christian culture. "What about the Crusades?" they say.

These days, the word *community* is almost "wheelhouse-esque" in its overuse. Jesus' contemporary followers break community with astonishing ease. A quick glance at the denominational breakdowns within the Christian church testifies to that. Modern technology and myriad options allow us to inhabit spiritual and cultural echo chambers in which we only ever encounter people with the same interests and affectations as us. When things get dicey, a change is just a click away. It seems many people realize true community is lacking in our culture, in our neighborhoods, and in our churches, yet fail to understand what community means in the first place.

As church attendance declines, however, an interest in the small, the communal, and the handcrafted seems to be increasing everywhere I look. Could it be that a generation defined primarily by its consumption habits—a generation with a product for every perceived need—is feeling duped? My generation and the one following mine are simply doing what we have been trained to do—to search for the meaning in our consumerism. We use products to define our values. We make statements with our debit cards. We vote by spending our money in specific ways. I do believe, however, that we can transcend this habit. Maybe we can even redeem it.

In the fourth chapter of his gospel, the disciple John tells of a woman traveling alone in the heat of the day (probably to avoid drawing the judgment of the other women who would make that journey in the morning or evening) to draw water from an ancient well. Jesus is breaking a slew of cultural tenets and religious laws when he engages her, and despite her brokenness — or maybe because of it — he connects her physical thirst to a deeper need and then offers to satisfy this need eternally. Jesus offers the living water that meets our every need — including the needs we don't even realize we have. Industrialized religion offers us neatly bottled water and carefully manufactured, bite-sized bread instead — just enough to leave us knowing we have to come back tomorrow for another bite, until the day comes when we stop making our way to the well at all and stay home to watch TV instead.

John tells us that Jesus' countercultural interaction with that woman of ill repute led not only to her belief in him as the Anointed One, but that many other Samaritans came to faith as a result. These people, despised by the religious elite of the day, recognized something in Jesus that the priests and teachers of the law did not. Sure, there was regular water in that ancient well, but there was also a more important truth at work. I am finding a similar kind of deeper truth rippling beneath the surface of the artisanal, handcrafted, small-batch culture shift spreading across the developed world.

In my neighborhood, we have five independent coffee shops but not a single Starbucks. I have a friend who makes chocolate that costs ten times more than Hershey's, and he can barely keep it in stock. Though he does not emblazon his bars with Bible verses or sell them in church gift shops or Christian bookstores, for him, chocolate is spiritual. There's a microbrewery in Nashville named after—and clearly inspired by—the theology and community celebrated by Martin Luther a half millennium ago, and another brewery out in the country that is run by two Catholic brothers who made their first batch of beer for a family wedding. Jesus is a role model for them. Then there's John, a master artist in pastries, cakes, and breads, who chose to close his family-operated shop instead of cheapening it the way profit realities and market forces dictated. Yes, there are important truths to be discovered in my neighborhood, at this table. There's a fingerprint here just waiting to be discovered. I believe these things can be signposts pointing us to the kind of soul-satisfying meal that will ruin us for the cheap, mass-produced stuff.

When I was thirteen, reeling in fear, self-doubt, anger, and a growing bitterness, I read *Mere Christianity* by C. S. Lewis. While the book is full of zingers, one line in particular struck me. "If I find in myself a desire which no experience in this world can satisfy," Lewis wrote, "the most probable explanation is that I was made for another world."* That's it! I'm hungry for

---

*C. S. Lewis, *Mere Christianity* (New York: Macmillan, 1943), 120.

something that this world in its current, broken state can't yet offer me. I'm thirsty for water from a deeper well.

Are you?

I needed a trail out of my own hunger and into the true banquet of God's goodness. I didn't see the connection between my musical passions, my growing interest in cooking and crafting, and how my faith was evolving. It took two years of work on this very book to come to terms with the idea that this fascination with resurgent spiritual values coming through the artisanal fringes of our culture is directly connected to my own story. Pulling back curtains often leads us into a new awareness of the beauty we have been numbed to for too long.

EVERYTHING IS SPIRITUAL

For as long as I can remember, everything has seemed spiritual to me. I notice ripples all around me, like the expanding circles from a stone thrown into a pool generations ago. I've seen the fingerprint of God in the night sky, a pigpen, a bumblebee, and the bite of an Illinois winter day. Sometimes I laugh at myself when I think this way. *See that weed growing through the crack in the driveway?* I ask myself while dejungling my yard. *That weed is like evil—finding a crack to grow through. Or maybe the weed is the truth—the inexorable push of light and life into hardened places.* So, yes, I may be an expert in overanalysis.

These are the types of things I'm contemplating when I get that far-off look. It may be silly, but I like to think I'm in good company. Jesus used common metaphors and symbols constantly. While humans can be incredibly obtuse, God seems to actually want us to uncover these critical, life-changing truths. He knows how oblivious we are, and he has sprinkled signs, guides, and tokens all over our paths.

Though God's face was often obscured by my confusion, pride, and pain, I can't remember a time when I didn't believe in him. I may not have understood him, but I was sure he was there. I remember being furious at him, but also being unable to shake him. I've tried being a skeptic, to imagine life as an elaborate accident. Then a song would come on, and I'd be struck by the intentional extravagance of art. I've gone through many a season feeling worn-out, frustrated, or even ashamed of "The Church," yet I've experienced firsthand the life-saving power of sacred community. I've found a supernatural reservoir of grace that has allowed me to forgive terrible wrongs, and to be forgiven. I've seen, tasted, heard, smelled, felt, and experienced too many wonders to ever accept that life is an accident. But that doesn't mean I've figured it all out.

It is heartbreaking to see so many people missing out on these rhythms. Thousands—maybe millions—of young people have religiously plugged "tab A" into "slot B" all their lives, only to be left feeling empty and let down. They've avoided all the bad things in life, done their Christian duty, rinsed and repeated. But sometime in their twenties or thirties, they start to feel as though it's all a ploy—or worse, a product. In some cases, they're right; in other cases, they simply got off on the wrong foot.

In the book of Genesis, we read the ancient accounts of Adam and Eve, Cain and Abel, Noah, Abraham, and others who hear directly from God yet still manage to blow it. In the book of Judges, we encounter God's wayward sons losing sight of the plot amid the transition from the Bronze Age to the Iron Age, just a generation after Joshua's death. The Middle Ages brought us the Crusades and the various Inquisitions. Theological error and extremism are obviously not limited to any particular era, but the effects of the Industrial Revolution are often far less appreciated than those of earlier epochs. Perhaps that is because we are currently still trapped in their grip.

For the purposes of this conversation, I conveniently lump manufacturing, mass communication, global transportation, the Internet, and modern free-market capitalism under the heading of "industrialism." We have seen our culture move from being largely agrarian and artisanal to one of Facebook, Walmart, and Amazon.com in a matter of a couple of centuries. That's breakneck speed, sociologically speaking. It's worth considering the implications.

Our industrialist culture is exceptionally good at shaping and reinforcing what I call the "sacraments of progress":

- consistency
- customization
- measurability
- efficiency
- progress
- guaranteed satisfaction

Sacraments, when properly applied, reinforce values. They show on the outside what is happening on the inside. Baptism shows we are sharing in the death and resurrection of Christ and are a part of his body. Marriage, with all of its ceremony and symbolism, is simply the outward demonstration of a change in the hearts of a couple. They may look like two individuals, but they have spiritually become "one flesh." When we share the Eucharist (or take Communion), we eat bread and drink wine as outward signs of something profoundly important that is happening on the inside. We are partaking in the body and blood of Christ — bringing it into ourselves in one of the greatest mysteries of the faith. Sure, many people move lightly through the process or see it as superstitious or abstract, but the essence is there for anyone who desires to experience it.

The "sacraments of industrialism" have similarly formed and reinforced the values many of us unwittingly live and define ourselves by. Our primary identity is that of producers and consumers of goods. The customer is always right, so when we are not satisfied, we should switch brands. The goodness of a thing is determined by how well it "works." Bigger is almost always better, in one way or another. The winners make the rules. The bottom line is our king. Conformity is a virtue. Our society reinforces these values constantly through the marketing we imbibe, the stories we tell, and the songs we sing. We are what we do. We're entitled to comfort, stimulation, and satisfaction. The Factory, functioning as the church of industrialism, is efficient at satisfying our wants because it invests considerable energy in shaping them. It seems the advances in technology that resulted from the invention of the assembly line were nothing compared to the Industrial Revolution's ability to reframe our identity as human beings. In fact, all the Revolution did was pour lubricating grease on the greed, fear, and violence native to our hearts. Industrialism isn't responsible for our destruction; it simply accelerates it.

This is the world we inhabit. And while I'm all for cultural relevance, when the apostle Paul said that when he was in Greece he was a Greek, I don't think it included indiscriminately taking on the underlying values of contemporary Greek culture. At Mars Hill, Paul demonstrated a conscious awareness of those values, but there is no indication he embraced them. In fact, the power of the true gospel is that it transcends culture. We thus have the opportunity to live in a mysterious paradigm in which we are in the world but not of it.

When left on our own to define what being "of the world" means, we create millions of different sets of rules. There are some obvious ways to be "of the world" that the church universally acknowledges and rightly rebukes. Murder, theft, rape, and greed are clearly vices that take us further from God's heart. But what about subtler practices? What about consumerism that creates victims in the developing world? What about the kind of entertainment that objectifies human beings, who are created in the image of God? What about "sanctified" ministry projects that pull millions of dollars away from the poor? What about seemingly reasonable money management programs that ensure we will retire wealthy but don't include caring for our neighbors?

Sure, there are blatant ways in which the world flaunts its lawless, loveless ways and tempts us to satisfy our desires at any cost. But what about those socially acceptable practices that look "normal" or even "Christian" yet subtly fuel destructive tendencies? Which is more dangerous — a city like Las Vegas that unapologetically deifies the self and makes a sacrament of satisfaction, or a church full of self-serving, highly marketed, consumerist Christians who aren't even aware of the ways in which their lifestyles are feeding the Factory far better than they are feeding the Good Shepherd's sheep? These are the questions that have haunted me for a long time. When I examine my own actions, I am troubled by how many of them are driven by my own wants and are shaped by my culture far more than they are inspired by the words, work, and person of Jesus.

Even a casual look at our modern Christian culture reveals myriad ways in which these mass-market values of industrialism — these sacraments of progress — have shaped the formation of our rituals, our worship, our behavior, and our values. We adopt worldly, corporate definitions of success and live out our faith accordingly. And now, as the tenets of consumerism and capitalism teeter, and creation groans in pain as we wring out every last natural resource in our search for comfort, it should come as no surprise that young people are bailing out. This "product" called Christianity just isn't working.

CRAFTED, NOT MANUFACTURED

A linguistic code is evolving for differentiating mass-produced, manufactured goods from handmade fare. Using the word *craft* or *crafted* implies a level of skill or excellence that comes from extensive experience, practice, and training. The word *artisan* implies a level of creativity or artistry that takes this kind of craft to another level. To that end, anything can be crafted rather than manufactured. Crafted food is put together by hand, not assembled in a factory. Craft beers are made in small batches with carefully chosen ingredients. A book, song, or film can be intentionally and soulfully crafted or, like a paint-by-number project, can simply be thrown together by machine, based on a template.

When something is crafted instead of manufactured, it often costs more. It will generally be unique—even eccentric. Craft-roasted coffee will taste slightly different from batch to batch. Craft or home-brewed beer will taste different based on slight changes in water chemistry or how long a certain ingredient was allowed to boil. Major manufacturers like Budweiser, Coke, and Starbucks invest millions of dollars into the tools and technologies needed to make their products look, smell, and taste the same everywhere. While there is certainly something to be said for this kind of expertise, many people actually crave the unique touches that only handcrafted items can deliver. When it comes to aspirin or car tires, predictability and consistency are critical. When it comes to food and drink and textiles, however, slight variations and nuances keep things interesting. And when it comes to the formation of our faith and values, an artisanal approach—one that includes master and protégé intentionally crafting something from God-given materials in a way that works because it is true—may be something that can actually change the world. As you'll see in these pages, this is the process that is changing me right now.

In ancient times, the evolution of the town and city allowed people to become experts (artisans) and then to trade the fruits of their labor for other things they needed or wanted. The manufacturing and distribution technology developed during the Industrial Revolution allowed more items to be manufactured, and the prices of those items dropped substantially. The artisanal movement has reintroduced premodern, handcraft techniques but serves them up at specialty prices. Modern manufacturing (along with government subsidization of factory farming) has made food cheaper than ever before, relative to other costs of living. This phenomenon has led Americans in particular to expect to spend very little of our available income on food. As the artisanal movement gains momentum, millions of people are deciding that the nutritional, environmental, and moral benefits of small-batch, local, handcrafted foods are actually worth the extra expense.

The choice often comes down to convenience and low prices versus craft and excellence. The same potential dichotomy exists in the theory and practice of the Christian faith. The question lingers: Was the ministry and message of Jesus more in line with an artisanal and carefully crafted ethic, or a cheap, one-size-fits-all approach?

At the obvious risk of deifying a different kind of consumption, I believe there are signs of life all around us. I regularly encounter people who are doing their best to reverse the effects of industrial "progress"—at least in their own hearts and minds. There are twentysomethings who shop each week at farmers markets, thirtysomethings who play in string bands, teenagers who collect vinyl LPs. The resurgence of premodern values that has brought back backyard gardens, true home cooking "from scratch," and an appreciation of handcrafted goods encourages my soul. Sure, much of it is surface-level hipsterism at best, but the underlying values that propel this movement are compelling.

Examples abound: Quirks and anomalies are now cool and are prized instead of corrected or homogenized. Customers are starting to realize they aren't always right and may need to be inspired and reeducated. Some things are worth extra investment; cost is not the only indicator of value. Ancillary factors related to environmental impact, human exploitation, health factors, and accessibility are relevant to a thing's "goodness." Smaller is often better. There is much more to "success" than profitability. Some things don't "scale" without compromising their nature. If something is good, we need to *make* it work.

Many who identify with these values consider themselves quite spiritual, even though they're not the slightest bit interested in "organized religion." If Jesus' response to the organized religion that set up tables designed to exploit the poor and the weak in the Jewish temple is any indication, I think it's safe to say that Jesus himself was not much of a fan of industrialized faith. When functioning properly, however, the body of Christ can accomplish amazing things—things individuals could not accomplish on their own.

Now, to be clear, I still desperately believe that the church, the worldwide community of faith, despite so much historical and current evidence to the contrary, is the great hope of the world. Before Christianity became the law of the land in Rome—before the dawn of Christendom—the church was a ragtag group of socially radical troublemakers that grew in number despite horrific persecution. The church grew because people were drawn to the words and the actions of its members. They had no candidates in elections, no commercial appeal, and certainly no buying power. They did, however, have hearts full of self-sacrificial love and a willingness to change their ways. They loved the unlovely. They cared for the poor, the orphan, and the widows. Their actions defied human nature. Their power came through human vulnerability infused with the supernatural power of the Holy Spirit. The world noticed. Some sang along, and some started gathering up these Jesus people and burning them at the stake.

There is something beautiful and counterintuitive about the selflessness provoked by a true understanding of the words and work of Jesus. Christians have been a force behind abolishing slavery, promoting workers' rights, literacy, disaster relief, adoption, poverty relief, and even environmental preservation. The church has taken its share of black eyes—often well earned—but followers of Jesus have also made the world much better for millions of people.

Religion has been used as a tool by hateful people, but that says more about the people using it than the essence of the gospel itself.

So yes, all this may be the ramblings of a madman obsessing over a plateful of potatoes, desperate for them to mean something. I suspect, however, that there is more going on here than just another fad. As I, and millions like me, search for something more meaningful in our coffee, bread, beer, and chocolate, I sure hope we find it. I would love for these conversations and those yet to happen to inspire church leaders to dare to rebuke the relentless seduction of progress and growth. I'd love to encounter a rich, satisfying, whole grain, hand-hewn gospel being lived out in churches from coast to coast. Regardless of what happens on an institutional level, however, I am confident that when these values are applied to the cultivation of our individual spiritual lives, within the context of our local communities, the results will be profound. One of the most consistent truths about human nature—one of the tenets most threatening to corrupted systems of power—is that real change happens at the ground level.

Chapter 3

BREAKING BROKEN BREAD

*J*ohn Jasiak and I were hanging out in the kitchen of my Aurora house one wintry night in the late 1990s as our kids played together and our wives visited in the front room. John had brought a couple of brown paper bags with him, and history had taught me that whatever was in those bags would be amazing. I was not disappointed.

John owned Krupicka's, a traditional Bohemian bakery in the western suburbs of Chicago where, along with his father, he crafted some of the best breads and sweets I have ever tasted. While the "Bohemian" in his credentials clearly referred to baking traditions originating in the central European region known as Bohemia, the hippie/free-thinking connotations applied as well. John was a trim, long-haired Christian who spent many evenings and weekends playing in a rock band with his brother and some friends. Cast aside whatever mental picture you may have in your mind of a rotund, ruddy-faced baker. Picture Joe Satriani dusted with flour, and you'll be closer to the truth.

John brought baked goods with him wherever he went—sweet cinnamon apple breads, rye bread, rolls, and his family's famous kolaches. On one of the most difficult nights of my life—the night my music store and concert venue True Tunes had its farewell bash—John made an amazing black cake, complete with a drum set, amps, and microphones. He was a genius with flour, eggs, and yeast, and while you could tell he took great pride in his work, he was consistently humble and generous. Though his band was good, it was clear that John's primary vehicle of artistic expression was his oven.

The conversation John and I had that night in my kitchen planted seeds that have grown in my heart and mind, eventually changing the consistency and texture of my whole life. After tasting a bit of his sticky apple bread, I just had to know how he made it. As he told me how he combined old-world recipes with his own creative experiments, I was transfixed. John was doing with flour what my favorite musical artists were doing with music. He had a deep reverence for the traditional ways but just enough rock-and-roll swagger to dare to kick things up a notch. I was just starting to get more interested in cooking, and I found John's craft fascinating. I kept drilling him for information long after we had surpassed my realm of comprehension. He was talking about types of flour, rising times, different leavenings, and how it all comes together. I was nodding along as if I understood completely.

Something he said stopped me in my tracks. "Factories have only been making bread, slicing it, and sticking it into plastic bags for fifty years or so," he said. "For most of human history, everyone either made bread like this at home or bought it at a local bakery." Supersoft, long-lasting, plastic-wrapped, and sliced have been the dominant forms of bread in my lifetime. It seems as if it has always been that way, but it has not. I immediately thought about the manufactured, presliced, plastic-wrapped, self-help spirituality that largely defines Western Christianity these days. Many people reject that kind of gospel precisely because it seems so processed and fake. Worse, others develop such a taste for theological Wonder Bread that they can't stand the texture, flavor, or color of the real stuff.

John then told me, in general terms, about the history of the industrialization of bread and where his techniques fit into the story. It was enough to spark more curiosity on my part. I started digging.

DAILY BREAD: THE DAWN OF COMMUNITY

Historians connect the discovery of both beer and bread with the dawn of civilization. Early humans were hunter-gatherers who lived on a diverse diet of greens, seeds, nuts, berries, meat, fowl, and fish. Although this history predates any written records, archaeologists believe the discovery of what could be done with grains—notably brewing and baking—caused people to create permanent settlements and to cultivate cereal crops. There are some who believe beer came first, and that bread was simply beer gone wrong, but no one knows for sure.

While certainly a positive advancement in many ways, the formation of settlements and villages is an early example of a culture trading quality (nutritional in this case) for convenience and comfort. The diverse diets of the hunter-gatherers were likely far healthier but required great risk, hard work, uncertainty, and travel. The cultivation of cereal crops provided security, predictability, and relative ease. Bread and ale were moderately nutritious, naturally fermented, and locally grounded. While for Europeans and Africans these crops tended to be wheat and barley, the same process happened in Asia with rice, and in the Americas with early versions of corn. Each culture developed its own version of flatbreads and ales, followed by leavened and refined breads and cakes.

For thousands of years, then, bread was made daily — whether in the home or by a local specialist. The processes of brewing and baking cause chemical changes in the grains used, rendering them digestible by humans. Without exposure to heat and moisture, the sugars stored in each kernel of wheat or barley would pass right through the human digestive tract. A combination of experimentation, artistry, and what certainly seemed like magic led to everything from Celtic oatcakes to Indian naan bread, Egyptian ta bread, Mexican tortillas, and Jewish matzah.

Bread frequently takes center stage in the story of the relationship between God and humankind. Prior to the exodus of the Hebrew people from Egypt, God gave specific instructions on the type of bread his people were to make and eat. In Exodus 12, God required the people of Israel to make bread without yeast. Once Pharaoh finally decided to allow the Hebrew people to leave Egypt, they had to move quickly. Yeast takes time to work through a lump of dough, causing it to rise. By making the dough unleavened, they could carry it with them immediately.

After their release from Egypt, the people of Israel grumbled against God and complained to Moses that they would have been better off under Pharaoh's hand. Although they were enslaved in Egypt, at least they had food to eat. Exodus 16 tells us God heard their grumbling and provided a supernatural source of sustenance for them. This mystical "manna" appeared with the morning dew six days a week and disappeared in the heat of the day. Manna is described as being flaky and white and tasting "like wafers made with honey" (Exodus 16:31). God instructed the Israelites to gather only what they needed for each day, trusting him to provide nourishment daily. However, some chose to gather extra portions, not sure whether they could trust God to continue to provide. When they did, the manna spoiled. When God told them to gather a double portion on the sixth day so they could honor the Sabbath, some chose to try to gather manna on the seventh day, only to find it didn't arrive.

The story of manna in the desert tells us much about the nature of God and the importance of bread. He did not give his people bitter, tasteless bread. He did not ration the amount they could eat, just the amount they could store. Numbers 11 tells us God allowed them to bake it into loaves or boil it into a sort of porridge. It's reasonable to think they found creative ways to prepare manna during the forty years they ate it. While this story about manna reminds us of humanity's fear, selfishness, forgetfulness, vanity, and ungratefulness, ultimately the story is about God's provision, his mercy, and his faithfulness. The manna in the desert is a precursor of the ultimate bread God would one day send his people—Jesus.

A GIFT OF BREAD

My wife and I frequently joke that God must really not want us to have any more resources than we actually need. As a result, we've been blessed by the generosity of others more times than I can count. Once, just before we got married, we were completely out of cash. We were the "no money for food" kind of broke. One night when I brought Michelle back to her apartment, we found several bags of groceries by her front door. This kind of thing has happened more than a few times. I've always wondered how winning a Grammy Award can be humbling; accepting food because you're broke is humbling.

It's relatively easy to declare that money isn't important when you're nineteen years old. Michelle and I agreed that people, ministry, music, and family were the priorities for us, and if that meant we didn't reach our full earning potential— ever—that would be OK. When we were first married, I was a couple of years into my True Tunes experience, running a record store, booking bands, writing about music, and living on about a thousand bucks a month. As the babies started coming and we chose to have Michelle stay home with them, our commitment to this ministry-oriented lifestyle was tested. We rarely had any money left over at the end of the month. We were never able to put much in savings. Sometimes—even when we told no one we were struggling—friends took it upon themselves to bless us. Those gifts always came right on time, usually right when I started stressing. But even though God has provided for us through his people time after time, I have never really learned to count on it.

When we occasionally find ourselves with some extra money, we have learned to hold on to it for a minute and wait for something to break or flood, or for someone to get sick. After nearly twenty-five years of this, you'd think I'd feel deep down in my heart and know in my mind that God is good and that the choices we've made are good and true. You'd think that seeing our four children grow into passionate, creative young adults would be enough. You'd think another bag of groceries or a surprise cash gift of a thousand dollars during a particularly trying month would be proof we are well cared for. But like the Israelites, I often find myself grumbling about manna and asking God for some quail to go with that. And then a burger.

Years ago, when we were living in the Pigeon Hill neighborhood on the east side of Aurora, Illinois, I was stressing about how we were going to make ends meet that month. It was a Saturday morning, and my business was in the process of shutting down and I wasn't being paid my full salary. I went out on our little front porch and found a small paper bag. In it was a loaf of crusty, grainy bread that seemed to be a sourdough rye. I couldn't believe it. I took it inside and cut off a chunk. It was tough, but rich tasting. It reminded me again of manna — of God's provision of daily bread.

We later found out that George, an elderly man who lived a few doors down, had given us that bread. George had been born in our neighborhood some eighty years earlier. He walked past our house several times a day on his way to the Romanian Orthodox church around the corner. George was a deeply spiritual man. He was the only remnant I knew of the large Romanian community that had settled in our neighborhood after World War I. He was sweet, sincere, always eager to have a conversation, and genuinely in touch with Jesus. I learned from him that placing bread on someone's doorstep was an old Romanian tradition of blessing. When I thanked him for the gift and told him it reminded me that God was always looking out for us, he grew a bit teary-eyed. "I say a prayer of blessing whenever I leave a gift of bread on someone's doorstep," he said. "I rarely hear anything about how those blessings affect people." I miss George. I want to be George to the people in my life.

The following Christmas I had an idea. Since our neighborhood was mostly Mexican at the time and I was a fan of all things Mexicana, our family prepared a batch of homemade sweet tamales, a traditional holiday corn bread treat native to the part of Mexico our neighbors came from. On Christmas Eve, we knocked on a few doors, sang a Christmas carol, and offered a plate of pineapple raisin tamales to our neighbors. It was a good night.

THE WORD BECAME BREAD

Although there is nothing inherently evil about yeast, it is often used as a symbol of sin and corruption in the Old and New Testaments. In Matthew 16, Jesus uses bread as an object lesson about corruption and false teaching. After refusing to give the Pharisees and Sadducees (the religious rulers of the day) "a sign from heaven" to prove he was the Messiah (verse 1), Jesus warns his disciples (verse 6) to be on their guard against "the yeast of the Pharisees and Sadducees." He then patiently explains that his frustration with the corruption of these religious leaders isn't so much about bread as it is about bad ideas and bad teaching—the "yeast" taking over the good "bread" of the gospel.

In his first letter to the church in Corinth, the apostle Paul uses the metaphor of leaven (yeast) to represent sexual sin that had crept into the church and needed to be addressed. In this case, the sin involved a type of incest—a man sleeping with his father's wife. Whether she was his biological mother is not specified, but Paul clearly says this is a kind of sexual immorality "even pagans do not tolerate" (1 Corinthians 5:1).

These examples and the many others that appear in Scripture capture the central theme of God's relationship with humanity. The manna, the unleavened bread of the exodus, the detailed instructions God gave Moses for making ceremonial bread, and the loaves and fish miraculously provided by Jesus to large crowds of hungry people (Mark 6:32–44; 8:1–10) all emphatically point to Jesus. People need to eat, and bread is good to eat. But there is something deeper, something profoundly subversive, about God's use of bread in the ongoing conversation he has with his people. There is something we need much more than food.

John 6 details the real point of all the bread talk that has come before. Crowds of people are following Jesus around, hearing of miracles and catching bits of the teaching that set this carpenter-turned-rabbi apart from anyone they had ever heard. He turned water into rich wine at a wedding party. He offered eternal life to the Samaritan woman at the well. He healed a royal official's son with just a word from his mouth. He got in trouble with the religious leaders by healing people on the Sabbath. He said things about himself that had to be considered blasphemy if they weren't true. He proclaimed his unity with God and pronounced judgment on the religious hypocrites who would condemn him. We may like to imagine Jesus as a soft-spoken healer who just wanted to get along with everyone. He does not give us that option. In John's account, Jesus draws a line in the sand. The claims he makes, as C. S. Lewis detailed in *Mere Christianity*, demand that we dismiss him as a lunatic, lock him up as a fraud, or worship him as Lord of all.*

And the central image he uses to describe his nature, his purpose, and his authority is that he is, of all things, the "bread of life."

> *Jesus said to them, "Very truly I tell you, it is not Moses who has given you the bread from heaven, but*

---

*C. S. Lewis, *Mere Christianity* (New York: Macmillan, 1943), 56.

it is my Father who gives you the true bread from
heaven. For the bread of God is the bread that comes
down from heaven and gives life to the world."

"Sir," they said, "always give us this bread."

Then Jesus declared, "I am the bread of life.
Whoever comes to me will never go hungry, and
whoever believes in me will never be thirsty.

JOHN 6:32–35

Bread marked the dawn of civilization, and bread will save
it. The interaction of human creativity and discipline with
the chemical elements God vested into various grains and
into the wild yeasts that blow unseen in the wind combine to
create countless flavors, textures, colors, and aromas. Bread
differentiates cultures, fills stomachs, and brings happiness
and contentment. Bread is security. God designed bread for
both temporal and eternal purposes. Like the five thousand
men gathered on that seaside hill two millennia ago,
however, we often seek the most expedient way to fill our
bellies while we miss the bigger picture. John tells us many
in the crowd were ready to crown Jesus king, not because he
could deliver them from their sin, but because he could meet
their immediate need for food.

I think many Christians, me included, continue to do exactly
that. When we feel Jesus is meeting our immediate needs, we
dig him. We want him at our party. We call him Lord, like
misogynistic rappers at the Grammy Awards. But when he
shares bread with us that is chewy, challenging, and hard to
swallow, we spit it out. I have prayed for an end to poverty,

only to be immediately confronted with my own selfishness. I have negotiated with God like a tenth grader on exam day: "Please, Lord, help me in the way I want to be helped, and I promise to make you King of my life." I can almost always sense the right thing to do, the way of truth and light and love. But I'd rather take the easier, sweeter, softer path.

The bread Jesus offers is his body, broken for me. It has the power to change me from the inside out — to nourish my soul, mind, and spirit in ways I can't understand. I have tasted that kind of nourishment. I have felt it course through my veins and up my spine. But the sweet, soft taste of all of the counterfeits is still tempting. This is the tension the disciple must choose to embrace. This is the way love tastes.

BROKEN BREAD

If the first few thousand years of man's relationship with bread were about establishing communities and putting down roots, the last few hundred have been a study in how to remove everything of value from a kernel of wheat. During the Middle Ages, long before people understood much about germs, fungi, microbes, or anything else too small to be seen with the naked eye, it was widely believed that processed white flour was healthier than darker whole grain flours. This is because bread made with whole grain flour tended to become moldy faster than bread made with white flour. For centuries, white flour was associated with wealth and sophistication, while whole grain flour was relegated to use by the poor and simple. During the Industrial Revolution, commercial baking factories routinely added a wide range of chemicals and bleaching agents to make their bread softer, whiter, and more refined. It was during this era that, for the first time in human history, more people purchased bread commercially than baked it in their homes. Homemade bread became associated with backwoodsy, backward country bumpkins.

The processing of flour is all about technology. A kernel of wheat is composed of the bran (hard outer shell), the germ (the embryo of the seed), and the endosperm (the white starch designed to feed the embryo). Milling wheat removes the bran and the germ, leaving only the endosperm behind. The bran and germ, however, contain most of the nutritive value of wheat. Both are rich in fiber and healthy fats and thus make the grain more susceptible to spoilage than the endosperm alone. After removing these parts of the grain, what remains is a white, starchy, high-carbohydrate flour that is neutral tasting and easy to work with and to store. Medieval bakers noticed that the more they processed flour, the less likely it was to spoil quickly.

Although it would be another century before contemporary science and the United States government came to accept the nutritional facts about processed flour, in the early 1800s, a Presbyterian minister named Sylvester Graham (1794–1851) became an early proponent of whole grain foods, vegetarianism, and temperance. In 1829, he invented graham bread, a hearty loaf made of unsifted whole grain flour. His recipe serves as a precursor to the health foods of today. Later, Graham's flour was used to make crackers (yes, graham crackers), and while the medical and scientific communities of his day mocked him and corporate bakeries and meat processing companies castigated him, his avant-garde teaching, motivated in large part by his strident faith, was enormously influential on John Kellogg and other early critics of industrialized food. Graham believed the chemicals added to flour made it unhealthy—which later proved true. (His belief that vegetarianism was a cure for alcoholism—and even for impure sexual thoughts—was less viable.)

In the 1920s, nutritionist and biochemist Benjamin Jacobs, PhD, studied the nutritional effects of wheat processing and developed the first methods of adding lost nutrients back into manufactured foods. This "enrichment" had a substantial impact on the nutritional content of American and British foods during World War II and remains in effect to this day. Contemporary nutritionists, however, increasingly argue that while the artificial addition of chemical nutrients to processed flour is better than nonenriched, processed flour, the healthiest way to eat wheat is not to remove the bran and germ in the first place.

Whole grain wheat flour has become increasingly popular in American diets in recent years. Sadly, the demographics have flipped. Wealthy and educated people are far more likely to consume whole grain flour now, while low-income and less educated communities are more likely to consume diets high in processed white flour, sugar, and fat.

The removal of bran and germ from wheat does more than change the color and nutritional value. These components represent the most concentrated source of flavor in bread.

As with any food (other than sugar and salt, unfortunately), people must develop a taste for whole grain foods. A person raised on white bread will often find whole wheat too intense for their palate. Conversely, a person raised on whole wheat or someone who has taken the time to cultivate a taste for the richer flavor of whole grain will often find the flavor and texture of white bread unsatisfying. There is a reason "white bread" has become a cliché for anything that is mild, boring, safe, conservative, or plain.

Christians, especially evangelicals like me, often like to pulverize the gospel into small, fine, easy-to-digest particles. But if our creed can fit on a bumper sticker, we're doing it wrong. I believe this is a by-product of our well-intentioned and laudable desire to be understandable and relevant to our peers. In the process, however, we risk turning the Bread of Life into a Twinkie. At some point, the essence of the thing we are trying to sweeten is compromised beyond usability. This processed, refined gospel feels good going down and gives us a sugar rush of emotional energy, but when the buzz wears off, we are left with nothing but a headache. No white-bread gospel can satisfy the deep hunger of the human heart.

BAKING BREAD IN CHURCH

I've long been fascinated, bothered, and maybe even a bit obsessed about the kind of bread Christians use for Communion. In the more charismatic or evangelical churches of my childhood, we used big, chewy hunks of bread and ripped off our own pieces. In the Episcopal church, a priest served us superthin wafers that dissolved in our mouths without being chewed. One Baptist church I attended used tiny little flour pills that seemed more like cardboard Tic Tacs than anything resembling bread. At a Seder meal, which represented the actual Jewish ceremonial meal the disciples and Jesus shared at the Last Supper, we used matzah bread (think, unsalted crackers). While I certainly believe there shouldn't be only one acceptable type of bread used for this holy meal, matzah bread does seem to warrant some consideration.

In the sacred moment of the Eucharist, which is simply a Greek word for "thanksgiving," we are told that the unleavened bread Jesus served as a part of the Passover meal became representative of his body, given for us. This simple act is one of the great mysteries of the faith. The body of Christ crucified is the bread that comes from heaven and satisfies our ultimate need and deepest hunger. That bread, to me, deserves some respect.

We switched things up when we shared Communion at Warehouse Church in Aurora. Sometimes we used matzah bread. Sometimes we tore pieces off a communal loaf and served each other. On one Sunday when I was called on to lead this meal, I went to the Mexican bakery down the street and bought some freshly made bolillo rolls. The congregation liked that choice. Another Sunday, one of the pastors took it up a notch by bringing in a bread machine and baking fresh bread for Communion. The whole building was filled with a familiar enticing aroma. I remember feeling hungrier and hungrier as the sermon went on, longing for a taste of that bread.

Ultimately, I'm not sure there is a theological implication as to which kind of bread we consecrate for Communion, but I do think it is important to feel a hunger for that meal. If your participation in the Eucharist has become too casual or too habitual, open your heart and your mind to the reality behind the ritual. Whether it is a flour pill or a freshly baked hearth roll, realize that the Bread of Life is given for you, and remember the sacrifice made on the cross. Too often, I come to God's table with a belly full of junk food and a heart full of distractions. Beneath it all, though, I am ravenous for resurrection. I welcome all sights, smells, and sounds that help me remember real hunger and lead me to the only table that can truly satisfy it.

WHEAT TOAST ON A WINTER DAY

The years we lived on our central Illinois farm were dark years, to be sure. Still caught in the undertow of my biological father's presence, my mom did the best she could with her four little boys out there in the middle of nowhere. We were frequently the beneficiaries of governmental food assistance (read, welfare). In those days, welfare came in the form of actual food, not debit cards. I remember big blocks of "government cheese," as well as generic bags of flour, powdered milk, and canned meat. It was truly amazing what my mom could make with that stuff.

Our house was at the end of a quarter-mile driveway we called "The Lane." I swear, that stretch of gravel had a personality of its own. In the morning, my brother and I would walk that quarter mile to wait for the bus. Rural buses are unpredictable. Some mornings we would be running to catch it, while other days it seemed we sat out there for an hour. On winter mornings, my mom would fix us a warm breakfast of freshly baked wheat bread or homemade (whole grain) graham crackers spread with homemade peanut butter and accompanied by Tupperware cups of homemade hot chocolate. We would leave the cups in the mailbox at the end of the lane and bring them back to the house when we were dropped off in the afternoon.

Even though we were poor, my mother understood something about nutrition that other kids' moms didn't seem to get. White bread was rare in our home—and best used for French toast or grilled cheese, if it had to be used at all. Thus, my brothers and I saw white bread as a treat. On one of my first grocery shopping trips when I moved into my own apartment, I bought white bread.

My mom was also very strict about what we watched on TV. Out in the country, we were lucky to get two channels on most days. One was PBS, and the other was whatever channel aired *Three's Company*. I remember because we were not allowed to watch that show. During the first week in my own apartment, I noticed that one of the cable channels was airing a *Three's Company* marathon. I got my white bread, made a cheese sandwich or two, and sat down to watch as much *Three's Company* as I wanted.

I made it through an episode and a half and started feeling sick. Really sick. The white bread in my gut danced with the frustration and disgust I felt from having invested forty-five minutes in that show. I threw the bread out in the yard for the birds (apologizing to them as I did) and went to church.

Good food sustains us; bad food merely tides us over. I have grown up in a world full of processed, genetically modified, manufactured, plastic-wrapped bread while the good stuff resides at the margins, waiting to be discovered. Whole grain food is far more satisfying once you cultivate a taste for it. It fills you up with something other than sugar and empty calories. As my own kids head out into the world to work, to serve, to learn, and to leave their mark, I want to send them off with hearty whole wheat toast that will warm them from the inside out. I've got to get that recipe from my mom. In the most important ways, I already have.

HOMEMADE BREAD AND FRIENDSHIP: SOME THINGS DON'T SCALE

One of the most important accomplishments of industrialism is the value of scale. The assembly line is a truly amazing thing. Prior to this critical innovation, automobiles were only available to the rich. Once Henry Ford designed an assembly line to build cars, they became accessible to everyone. Similarly, once factory bakers learned how to automate the bread-making process and to prevent spoilage by removing the nutrients that bacteria and molds thrive on, they could scale up to meet the market's demand for convenience. Assembly lines changed manufacturing forever. They provided millions of jobs and made their owners fabulously wealthy. Our economy has become completely dependent on them. If factories disappeared tomorrow, millions of people would starve. Medications would disappear. The divide between those who can afford handmade cars, computers, and bread and the vast majority who cannot would increase exponentially. No, the answer is not to eliminate automation and the cost advantages of industrialism; it is simply to be more mindful of the things we subject to that process.

Scale makes food—and faith—cheaper than ever before. It is convenient and can be custom-designed based on our wants, desires, and lusts. Mass-market bread costs almost nothing. Get up close, though, and watch bread being made, and its value increases exponentially. Get your own hands covered in dough and invest precious time watching it rise and bake, and bread will be worth even more to you. The same is true when it comes to the community of faith. Millions of people attend some kind of church every Sunday, but it costs them nothing. Christianity might scale in the form of books, sermons, or gospel music, but discipleship requires close personal contact. Jesus addressed the crowds from time to time, but he spent much more time with his small group, allowing them to touch his hands and feet, to hear his words, and to see his tears up close and personal.

In many ways, Wonder Bread, the soft, white stuff that tastes exactly the same from coast to coast and around the world, serves as a perfect example of our species' worship of convenience, price, and scale. We've been conditioned to trade quality, flavor, and nutrition for ease and accessibility. We trade the truly good for the reasonably acceptable, whether in regard to our bread or our faith.

An artisanal baker can only produce a certain number of loaves per day if he is to remain committed to the integrity of his craft. Similarly, the human brain can only handle a certain number of active relationships. According to British anthropologist Robin Dunbar, this number ranges from 100 to 230, with a generally accepted average of 150. "Dunbar's number," as it is known, is based on a combination of archaeological evidence, psychological research, and physiological observation of the brain. Other researchers, using different methodologies, have come up with similar numbers. The general idea is that each of us only has the mental and emotional capacity to remain closely and meaningfully connected to a certain number of people. Technological tools such as spoken language and Facebook allow us to increase the total number of connections we maintain as we correspondingly decrease the level of connectivity we have with that network. The sociological implications are quite simple and plainly observable: the more people we know of, the fewer we truly know. Social scaling in the form of massive schools, large workplaces, churches, and now social networks such as Facebook, LinkedIn, and Twitter have extended our network into the thousands. The depth of those relationships, then, must be shallower. We simply can't be meaningfully connected to thousands of people. Science or not, I have certainly experienced this.

The artisanal movement inverts the economics of scale. Instead of "bigger is better," the microbrewer, local baker, indie band, or local coffee roaster thrives in a niche. Certain microbreweries, including the legendary Dogfish Head Brewery in Delaware, recently pulled their beer out of several states in order to meet the local demand without compromising quality. While the laws of scale may attempt to push any successful company to grow as large as it possibly can, Dogfish Head and other brewers have made the difficult decision to limit their growth—and shrink their customer base—in order to preserve the essence of the product they love.

How often do we encounter books, seminars, blogs, and discussions about church growth and hear that increased attendance is the evidence of God's blessing? When was the last time you heard about a church purposely choosing to say no to growth? The seduction of the big is so strong it has caught millions of Christians in its gravity. The problem is that authentic community is lost once the community becomes too large. Relationships necessarily become shallower. Eventually, many are left wondering what the point is of being part of a faith community, because they find it impossible to make deep connections within the massive crowd surrounding them.

The night we had some fifty people show up for our home group was a real learning experience for me. Our group had been steadily growing, and I had always been taught that growth was the natural result of life. If a community is thriving, it should grow, right? Not so much. That night, I wore myself out running from room to room and even running outside. I found a few folks in the driveway, wondering where to go. When it came time to pray for each other—one of the most important and nonnegotiable elements of our gatherings—we had to split into several groups so we could pray for everyone's needs. The biggest fail, though, was the fact that there were probably thirty people in attendance that night I wouldn't have been able to name. I had a sign-up sheet by the front door, and as I looked it over, I wasn't able to put a face to most of the names. "What just happened?" I asked Michelle.

Large groups can be easier to manage, because you can more conveniently skip the chewy stuff. A shallow group might remain intact longer because friction is greatly reduced when intimacy is limited by scale. I have friends who have attended megachurches for years without ever getting to know anyone. One friend said he loved going to a church of more than ten thousand people because it was like going to a hit movie or a big sporting event. He would see some familiar faces, shake some hands, and give some hugs— all of which scratched his itch for community. He would hear (consume) some good music, maybe watch a skit, and listen to some comedic church announcements and a thought-provoking, personally challenging sermon. There were more handshakes and hugs on the way out the door, possibly followed by a lunch gathering at a local restaurant. This guy was definitely a believer in Jesus. Eventually, he said he found it easy to skip out on Sundays. When he said he felt really disconnected and the relationships with his fellow churchgoers were mostly shallow, I asked him if he had been a part of any of the hundreds of small groups the church offered. "Never had the time," he said. I think he *did* have the time, but he never recognized the need. The "big church" experience was enough of a boost to get him through the week without any of the messy, difficult, or uncomfortable aspects of spending time with a small group of real people. "Big Church" offered him a reasonable facsimile, which allowed him to avoid the scary vulnerability of real community.

Many of us love the feeling of being on a winning team—the feeling that comes from attending a massively popular or respected church. But in my experience, the most critical reason to be a part of a church is for the personal relationships you can engage in and the opportunities church presents for serving others. Our current church is much larger than the church we attended in Aurora, but our small group ensures we remain intimately connected with a more manageable number of families. The Sunday experience, then, is about larger-scale corporate worship and teaching, which the church is exceptionally good at, and not the cultivation of deep friendships, which it can't possibly accomplish.

Some things are definitely better at scale. I'm sure glad we don't have neighborhood armies. I like that my hospital is big enough to have access to every possible specialist, lab, or other staff I might need. A small-town doctor probably wouldn't have had access to the people, expertise, or equipment needed when I had a life-threatening illness in 2006. I'm thrilled that the world's largest library—a collection of information that would have been unimaginable just twenty years ago—is now as close as my phone and feels relatively free. I know it was the size and scale of the company I work for that facilitated the free availability of worship songs around the world. When I traveled to a mountain village in Ecuador with Compassion International and heard children singing "Here I Am to Worship," a song written by English worship leader Tim Hughes for his local church, I knew it was technology and industry that facilitated the spread of that song. I'm no anarchist. Big can be awesome. But sometimes it's the last thing we need.

I was an early adopter of Facebook, and before that, I had a MySpace page. I remember the bizarre sensation of collecting "friends" on MySpace. I said yes to every invitation to connect. I like Facebook for what it is. I've been able to reconnect with old friends and to stay at least somewhat up to speed on the major life events of people I care about but don't get to see every week. I've discovered some cool records via the endorsements of people I respect, and I've gotten sucked into some crazy discussions about politics or theology that I actually enjoyed. Once, I found a friend of a friend for my sons to crash with when they went to an out-of-town concert. I certainly plan to use my extended network of Facebook contacts to get the word out about this book.

But there is a dark side to these massive social networks. There's the emotional lie that suggests I really have two thousand "friends" to validate my existence. Our world is full of so many irritations—with an ointment for every itch. The problem is that I have experienced many of those itches to be God-given reminders of my need for others, for peace, for faith. Hunger can drive me to seek out a healthy, satisfying meal, or to shove a Twinkie in my face. When I medicate the itch my heart feels for connection with a quick Facebook fix, I may lose out on the real thing my soul craves. The challenge, of course, is balance. Big, small, virtual, real, indie, industrial—I need to actively balance and moderate the voices that speak into my life. Eating some plastic-wrapped bread is much cheaper and much easier than baking my own bread for my sandwich, but ultimately not as satisfying.

BACK IN THE KITCHEN WITH JOHN

I reconnected with my baker friend John Jasiak recently. It took two years of digging to find him. It turns out that all a person needs to do to disappear in our culture is to refuse to create a Facebook profile. I was hoping to go visit his shop, certain that his artisanal approach to baking must be thriving in today's hipster climate. When I finally reached him by phone, his words broke my heart.

"I had to close the shop," he said. "It's been years now. We just couldn't keep doing things the way we wanted to and stay in business."

On a recent trip to Chicago, I met John at a local microbrewery to catch up, to hear his story, and to tell him about this book and his influence on it. Having lost a business built on my own dreams, I felt especially hurt by his news. I wanted to bake him a black cake — to return the favor. When I saw him, though, he looked great. His genuine smile was right there where it had been before, and his hair was still long.

John's bakery dream was inspired by his grandmothers — one Polish and one Italian. He started working at a family-owned bakery when he was sixteen, first washing the dishes and then working the mixer, the scale, the "bench," and eventually the oven. By the time he was twenty-three, his skills were polished. He could decorate a mean wedding cake. He opened his own bakery, where his mother and father worked in the evenings and the family offered up grandmotherly baked excellence to the community.

When John was a boy, the Jasiaks, like many Chicago families, were Catholics who went to church a couple of times a year. When he was about ten years old, his parents experienced a spiritual revival. His father had just lost his job when a neighborhood Baptist pastor knocked on their door. "My mom opened up the door, and a few minutes later, she was crying at the kitchen table. After they left, she said, 'Guess where we're going tomorrow? We're going to church!'

So we started going to a Baptist church—out of nowhere."
John made his faith his own a few years later, admitting that
for a while he had no idea what was going on.

The Jasiak family's faith was always central to the operation
of the bakery. Customers seemed to be looking for more
than baked goods. "People would come in crying," John
remembers. "We would listen, pray with people, and just
try to comfort them during hard times." The Jasiaks allowed
their faith to shine in how they treated their customers and
how they approached their work.

As time went on, however, it became increasingly difficult for
John to maintain his personal standards and to turn a profit.
As more and more people took to buying their baked goods
from grocery stores, the Jasiaks' customer base dwindled.
Everyone—especially European immigrants—adored their
old-world kolaches, but it was not enough to sustain the
business. When a Midwest distributor that supplied Costco
with baked goods approached John about making bundt
cakes, kolaches, and apple cakes, he thought it might be a
way to adapt. Corners had to be cut, ingredients changed,
packaging altered. Thinking it was his only hope for staying
in business, John made the changes. Right away, it felt
wrong.

"It was the beginning of the end," he says. "I still feel bad
about it. We had to make a decision to either bake for Costco
or go back to our old ways, which didn't work anymore,
either." The shop's customers were increasingly unwilling
to pay the kind of prices necessary to sustain the Jasiaks'

artisanal style. "Things were going down," John says. "People weren't buying sweets anymore. They started wanting artificial sweeteners. I prayed about it for about two weeks. I just couldn't go on like that. We either give it all up or we become a bakery for the big places. My mom said, 'What does this mean? What are you saying?' I said, 'We stop baking.'"

"I made a mistake," he says plainly. "I thought we could do it—and do it profitably. I was wrong." John sold the business to a competitor, handing over all of his regular customers and selling his equipment. When the new company asked for the family kolache recipe, however, he turned them down. He still bakes those amazing little cookies, as well as specialty breads and even big cakes—he does it in his home kitchen for friends and family instead. He bakes for love, not money. To pay the bills, he paints houses with his brother.

John still plays guitar in a band, but it's the worship band at his church now. He is at peace. He enjoys his life. He walked away from his dream instead of compromising it.

We all live somewhere between the Bread of Life and Wonder Bread. We desperately need the bread that sustains us, and yet we're so tempted by the convenient sugar high offered at the corner store. Learning to say no to the quick fix and to push my heart and soul to develop a taste for the good stuff has been one of the great challenges of my life. I can't walk past the bread aisle at the grocery store without thinking about the compromises I have made and the goodness I have passed up. The good stuff, whether we're talking about actual bread or all of the things it can represent, will take a little longer to get to and will cost a little more. In the end, though, I truly believe it's worth it.

Chapter 4

PURE CHOCOLATE

I remember one Christmas when I was about nine years old and my family lived on the farm. We'd had a terrible snowstorm and weren't able to travel to either set of grandparents' houses for the holiday. It appeared we were doomed to endure that late December alone in the bitter cold and snow. Somehow, a brave UPS man got his big brown truck down The Lane to deliver a large care package from my grandpa. My mom tried to convince us it was just some boring stuff we wouldn't be interested in. But the box was wet and falling apart, and from a tiny hole in one corner a small stream of M&Ms was leaking. My brothers and I lit up like Christmas trees. The box was clearly from heaven.

Since I was just a kid, chocolate seemed like a little love note from Jesus. Maybe it's because we usually got some at Christmas and in our Easter baskets. There were even a few Halloweens during the "satanic panic" that gripped evangelicalism in the late 1970s when my mom sent my brothers and me "tract or treating" instead of trick or treating. We handed out Christian booklets with little cartoons explaining that Halloween was evil but the reader could accept

Jesus into his or her heart right then and there by repeating a short prayer. We were given bits of candy in exchange, though I suspect most recipients of those tracts would have liked their candy back once they caught on to our tricky evangelism tactics. At the end of every Halloween adventure, my brother and I would pour our candy onto our beds and sort it in order of importance. Real chocolate was always the most prized.

Chocolate hints there is more to this world than meets the eye. It is made by people — artists — but of mystical ingredients God has hidden in remote jungles. Chocolate is the ultimate treat. All other candies pale in comparison. It goes with everything: cinnamon, mint, peanut butter, vanilla ice cream, fruit, nuts — even raisins. It comes in infinite forms and makes better everything it comes in contact with. The pictures painted of heaven as a place with streets made of gold have never been powerful for me, but the idea of an eternal supply of chocolate is enough to make me want to go.

It's a tragedy that so many people's impression of Christianity is that it is a culture of rules and prudes and austerity. In John 10, Jesus uses a story about a shepherd and his sheep to illustrate some profound truths about our true identity and God's intention toward us. After comparing sheep rustlers and thieves to the true protector and caregiver of the flock, realizing his audience is not grasping the meaning of his parable, Jesus makes one of the most profound statements in all of his sermons. "The thief comes only to steal and kill and destroy," he says. "I have come that they may have life, and have it to the full." That sounds extravagant. Like chocolate!

God's intention for his sheep is to protect and bless them, not to deny them. His law of love guides us to say no to some people, things, and ideas that come into our sheep pen, but not because he doesn't want us to have fun or enjoy our lives. When we are led to say no to one thing, it is always because our shepherd knows there is something better, richer, and more satisfying waiting for us. Like my mom, who would say I couldn't have a snack before dinner, Jesus doesn't want a quick, cheap snack to spoil our appetite for the feast he is preparing for us.

I was a kid who didn't have to look far to see that the world was broken. I didn't need a sermon to convince me things were not the way a good God wanted them to be. By age seven, I had a pretty good grasp of the concepts of sin and consequences. I knew about the thieves and sheep rustlers. I was pretty sure I understood hell. But chocolate, like music, whispered to me of another world.

AN APOLOGETIC FOR CHOCOLATE

Have you ever seen a cacao pod? Better yet, have you ever seen a cacao pod rotting in the sun? If you have, I doubt the first thing that came to your mind was "candy." Chocolate, like coffee, bread, and so many other essential human creations, is the product of a unique divine/human partnership. God gives us the raw materials and then allows us the pleasure and the honor of finding the way to make it taste good. Nature placed the cacao tree, with its leathery, seed-bearing pods, in Central and South America, and its secret treasures remained hidden for who knows how long. At some point, thousands of years ago, human artists started to interact with these beans—fermenting them, roasting them, grinding them, and combining them with other edible substances found in the forest. It was clear to the earliest cultivators of chocolate that this stuff was not of this world. It was called the "food of the gods" and was used as precious currency. It was sacred.

The creation of chocolate requires human interaction, creativity, persistence, and even artistry. Over the last couple of thousand years, this divine/human partnership has produced incredible results. This sacred food, once known only to a couple of Mesoamerican tribes, is now beloved around the world. It is savored by culinary experts, adored by children, physiologically and psychologically craved by women, and has even been turned into beer. For some, it is a treat; for others, it is an addiction. Artisans craft handmade expressions of it, and factories belch out millions of pounds into gas station candy racks. It's so ubiquitous and has become so accessible to the masses that it is easy to forget chocolate was once used in religious rituals and was available only to priests, nobility, and conquerors.

Chocolate has quite a biography. The earliest archaeological evidence of humans recognizing the value of the seeds of this funny little tree is found in Mayan carvings from around AD 300, but it was likely revered by ancient tribes more than a thousand years earlier. Interestingly, these carvings associate cacao seedpods with fertility, and they may be the earliest reference to chocolate's alleged aphrodisiac powers.

The Mayans created the first known cacao plantation on the Yucatán peninsula and used the seeds to make a cold, bitter drink. As they traded with the Aztecs, chocolate began its conquest of the world.

The Aztecs believed the cacao tree was brought to earth by their god Quetzalcoatl when he descended to earth on a beam of light, having stolen the tree from a garden in Paradise. They called its bitter brew xocolatl and believed it had medicinal and spiritual benefits. Cacao seeds were so prized in Aztec and other Mesoamerican cultures that they became a form of currency. By the fifteenth century AD, cacao (later anglicized as "cocoa") was a dominant cultural fixture of areas that currently range from the American southwest through Mexico and Central America and well into South America.

Christopher Columbus was the first European to encounter cacao when he landed in 1502 in what is now Nicaragua. He brought samples back to the king and queen of Spain and documented the use of the beans in Central American culture. But it wasn't until Spanish priests and monks began settling in the area that white people realized the true potential of the small seeds. Yes, Christian priests were the first global ambassadors for cacao.

But, of course, cacao couldn't stay spiritual. The Spanish conquistador Hernán Cortés was largely responsible for the real expansion of chocolate beyond Latin America. In 1528, he brought cacao beans and the tools used to create chocolate to King Charles V, suggesting it might be a good idea to combine cacao with sugar or other spices. Spanish cooks did just that, and they created the first sweet chocolate drinks. Cortés's discovery was a massive hit among the Spanish nobility. He then established his own cacao plantation in order to meet the new demand.

Chocolate remained Spain's secret for more than a century before it was introduced to France when Spanish princess Maria Theresa was betrothed to King Louis XIV in 1643. Within just a few years, chocolate—which by then had evolved into a form of candy and a sweet, warm beverage—exploded in popularity around Paris and London. Like the Mesoamericans, Europeans believed chocolate was an aphrodisiac. It was depicted by artists as an ultimate expression of decadence and pleasure. Chocolate's popularity quickly spread throughout Europe and the New World colonies.

Prior to the Industrial Revolution and the advent of the modern factory, chocolate was crude, messy, and extremely expensive. As technology improved, however, and as cacao plantations were established in the Caribbean, prices plummeted—and chocolate became available to the masses. Machinery and modern food science helped chocolatiers improve the smoothness, flavor balance, and durability of chocolate. Simply put, if not for industrialism and mechanization, the stuff we know today as chocolate would not exist—and whatever version was available would cost too much for most of us to afford.

There are many ways in which the relentless progress of technology makes our lives better—as we've seen with vaccines, highways, electricity, and air travel, among many other things. Progress, however, has no reverse gear or brake pedal. In the world of chocolate, this has led to hypermodern factories, chemical additives that allow candy bars to sit on store shelves for months—or even years—before being eaten, and relentless marketing designed to stoke demand.

This mystical food has also fueled and been fueled by human trafficking and slavery. The CNN Freedom Project suggests that hundreds of thousands of children across Africa are currently serving as slaves on cacao plantations. Over the centuries, millions of people have been enslaved in order to meet the developed world's hunger for chocolate. While the chocolate industry has recently made some moves to reverse this tragedy, there is a long way to go before the world's favorite sweet treat is no longer contributing to the objectification and abuse of human beings.

Nowhere is the zenith of chocolate more apparent than at the city-sized chocolate factory operated by Hershey's. The Hershey brand is nearly as iconic as its culinary cousin, Coca-Cola. Hershey's recently expanded plant in West Hershey, Pennsylvania, can crank out more than seventy million Hershey's Kisses per day, and in 2011, the company reported annual sales of more than six billion dollars. Hershey's also lends its name to dozens of different products—many of which have nothing to do with chocolate. Hershey's Syrup, for instance, is primarily made of corn syrup. Hershey's stands as a glowing example of American technological innovation, marketing prowess, distribution acumen, and corporate adaptation, if not culinary excellence. Hershey's chocolate is relatively low in actual cacao and contains numerous chemical ingredients designed to increase stability and decrease cost. For many, especially those who have had no exposure to artisanal or boutique chocolate, Hershey's has become the standard. It's not the best by a long shot, but it is definitely the biggest.

The sad truth is that chocolate has fallen from its sacred height. Most modern chocolate is cheap. Much of it is terrible. It scratches an itch in the same temporary way a cigarette does. It is designed to be gorged, not savored. It's not satisfying, interesting, surprising, or creative. It's a commodity. It's filler. It's killing people. The average American consumes twelve pounds of cheap chocolate each year. Mass-produced chocolate contains little to none of the nutritional value it could. It is more like a flavoring for sugar and fat. We crave it, we like it, we eat it—but rarely do we love it. It gets the job done. It's a sad shadow of its former glory, a faded Polaroid of a Monet. A new group of artisans, however, are doing their best to push back the bleak effects of industrialism on chocolate.

A CHOCOLATE PILGRIMAGE

Shortly after moving to East Nashville, my family discovered an event called the Tomato Art Festival. Hundreds of neighbors gathered together for music, an art show, various culinary experiments, and a generally good time under the hot August sun. I remember noticing beautiful retro posters announcing the presence of a new boutique chocolate company in our hood. I tried a sample. It had salt and pepper in it—but somehow, it worked.

A few months later, at a friend's party, I met Scott Witherow. "Scott owns Olive & Sinclair Chocolates," my hostess said. I felt like I was meeting the Wizard of Oz. "You make chocolate," I said enthusiastically. "That's amazing." I was finally meeting the man behind the posters and the samples. Somehow I knew we were going to hit it off. Our quick conversation revealed Scott was a believer who attended my family's church. Hearing just a few words from him about his craft showed that his passion was coming from a very deep and spiritual place.

Scott Witherow is a rising chocolate rock star. He's got the quiet awkwardness of an indie songwriter, the fashion flair of an accidentally hip farmer, and a sense of wonder and enthusiasm any poet would rightly covet. In the pursuit of purpose, meaning, and a career, Scott has traveled backward on the chocolate timeline, creating Olive & Sinclair Southern Artisan Chocolate in the process. In his search for honest, satisfying, and artistic chocolate, he also found God.

Olive & Sinclair's international headquarters are located in the basement of an East Nashville commercial building— approximately a mile from my home. Scott and I bumped into each other in the neighborhood, at concerts, and even at church. Our short conversations always ended with the Nashville favorite, "We have to get together some time." I watched as Olive & Sinclair grew, cheering Scott on all the while. Though I had no idea how to make chocolate, Scott felt like a kindred spirit. There was something about his pursuit of chocolate that resonated with me in a deep way. I finally got to sit in his tiny, cluttered office and hear about his journey. All around us were the sounds (loud) and smells (pungent) of world-class chocolate being made by a handful of young men and hand-wrapped in beautiful little labels by two lovely Mexican women. The fifteen-hundred-square-foot space in which Scott's employees work certainly isn't large enough to hold the waste Hershey's factory generates in mere seconds, but it is here that Scott's dream is becoming reality.

Scott grew up with a raging sweet tooth, a wandering heart, and a desire to cook. Though his parents encouraged him to start his higher education with a marketing degree, he eventually attended a prestigious culinary school and found himself cooking in some of the most famous restaurants in the world. He took to the culinary world quickly and completely. He worked at various gastropubs around London until one of his instructors landed him a job at the five-star foodie mecca called Nobu. One night, while Scott was immersed in his work, a patron with a different sort of accent came into the kitchen, pausing to chat with various chefs and watch them cook. Scott kept his head down and his eyes on his knife. Only later did he find out that Paul McCartney had been in the kitchen that night.

After finishing his studies and landing a variety of even more prestigious cooking gigs, Scott made his way back to Nashville. "Any time I got an opportunity to go work somewhere, I would go," he says. "I went to Birmingham and worked at Frank Stitt's restaurants for a couple days at a time. I was invited to go to Chicago and work at Alinea for a few weeks, so I did that. I went back to England for a few months to work at The Fat Duck in a small town outside of Windsor. Eventually, I came back to Nashville. I was the executive chef at The Trace for a while and the pastry chef at F. Scott's for years. I worked at The Wild Boar for a while."

Scott Witherow became the kind of chef who is recruited like an executive and booked like a rock star. He traveled around the world, earning recognition and money and living his dream. The problem was that he was never happy. "I had been married and divorced and hardly noticed," he admits. "I was probably more married to my work than I was to my wife."

Scott settled into a regular gig at F. Scott's in Nashville and was teaching pastry at the Art Institute of Tennessee, but he knew he was losing steam. Nothing was working.

FINDING A LIFE IN CHOCOLATE

Scott is a pursuer, a natural-born seeker. "I was just searching," he recalls. "My life has always been a search." As he felt the walls of home close in, he decided to travel around Canada with a friend. On a quiet street outside Toronto, Scott stumbled across a small "bean to bar" chocolate shop. He had bought unique chocolates around the world and had begun to wonder what it took to make chocolate. When he found someone actually making good chocolate, he was captivated.

Scott had found his calling. He returned to Nashville, quit his job, and announced that he was starting his own chocolate company. He collected vintage equipment and began making three-pound batches of chocolate in his apartment. The first results were terrible. Over time, through a lot of trial and error, Scott's understanding of the process improved. He found the necessary equipment, most of which was considered obsolete by modern chocolate makers. "I was surfing the Web to find out where you could buy small, old chocolate-making machines," he says with a pained laugh. "It's a lot easier now that I know where to go to find them. A stone grinder from 1900 isn't just something you can Google."

Scott's personal life started to settle down as well. He met a young woman named Aria at Nashville's Art Institute and felt an immediate connection. They were married in 2008, and Aria became an integral part of the launch of Olive & Sinclair. "It was good because Aria was a part of it from the very beginning," Scott says. "It was our thing, and not just my thing." He started to sense God's hand guiding him. "This whole time, God has told me where to go," he says, adding, "not that I always recognized it every time."

Scott's marketing education turned out to be a good investment. After noting that most chocolate labels lacked any real style, he connected with Bryce McCloud, a third-generation letterpress printer. This is where being a part of a creative community is a real asset. East Nashville is full of illustrators, designers, sculptors, chefs, painters, and producers. Based on the tagline "Southern Artisan

Chocolate," Scott and Bryce developed the now locally famous look and feel of Nashville's coolest new brand.

His first batch of commercially available chocolate was given away at the Tomato Arts Festival — the same festival where I first tasted it. Small, complimentary Olive & Sinclair bars were handed out far and wide. The labels looked great; the audience was primed. The only problem was that the chocolate was not good. "It was so bad," Scott recalls, "we had to add salt and pepper. The plain chocolate was so far from what I thought the flavor should be that I knew I couldn't serve it like that. So we decided to do something weird with it. I added salt and pepper, and it did the trick. It didn't make it taste like we wanted, but it made it passable." The Salt & Pepper Southern Artisan Chocolate bar is still available in local stores — East Nashville's favorite accident. Something that started out as junk is now a local delicacy.

Accidents became fewer and farther between, and Scott's culinary training and love of sweets eventually paid off in a big way. Olive & Sinclair is now one of the most acclaimed boutique chocolate companies in the United States. Critics rave about it; chefs at legendary restaurants use it in their dishes; microbreweries do craft-beer riffs with it; and customers in the region willingly pay seven dollars for a bar. This flies in the face of the prevailing assumption about American consumers — that cheaper is better. A Hershey's bar can be purchased for 80 percent less than one of Scott's concoctions, yet he can't keep up with the demand.

"I think it [Olive & Sinclair chocolate] is visually appealing to folks," Scott says. "They know it's handcrafted. It's built with the love of what we do. On top of that, our chocolate is as Southern and personable as it is good. We're the only chocolate makers who use brown sugar as our sole sweetener. We clean our beans by hand. We pick through them before they're roasted. They're loaded into the roaster by hand. They're loaded into the winnower by hand. Then they're stone-ground in a machine that was built before any of us were around. Those machines tell a story of their own! The upshot is that all of this translates into the flavor. I might be naive in that way, but I think it does."

Scott walks me through the shop—each station is just inches from the one before it. With a sound track courtesy of Kentucky rock band My Morning Jacket playing in the background, I watch as an employee holds a tray under a small spigot from which fresh, melted chocolate seeps. The bars that include extra ingredients—such as cinnamon and red pepper, sea salt, or roughly chopped locally roasted coffee beans—are doctored appropriately, then the racks are placed in a cooler to set. Later, they are hand-wrapped, first in foil, then in a dated and numbered paper label. "Every bar is dosed and hand-rattled through the cooling line, then hand-wrapped," Scott explains. "Everything that has been done to that bar has been done by hand. It's got to be a labor of love, because there are too many man-hours going into each bar!"

Scott recognizes that the increasing interest in supporting local business fuels the passion people have for his work. "People are starting to want to get food that's from their area. They want to get vegetables that are from within a fifty or hundred mile radius." The proximity cuts down on fuel consumption and ensures the product is as fresh as possible. "When someone buys one of our chocolates, they can see the exact date it was made," says Scott. "They can see it was made a week ago or maybe even a month ago, but not much more than that."

Ultimately, for Scott Witherow and the Olive & Sinclair crew, it's more about value than cost. "I think what we make is good," he says, "I don't think that about all chocolates. Once you taste it, you know the difference."

As Scott figured out chocolate making, other pieces of his life began to fall into place. Though he grew up in the church, and his parents' faith was a strong influence, his connection with God was sporadic. "I was raised to know God, and to want to know God," Scott says, "but I've been a wanderer. I was into rock and roll, and I got into some bad things living that chef life. But I always went back to God."

The mass-produced, prepackaged cultural Christianity of his youth left him hungry for something deeper, though — something authentic. There was no obvious moment of clarity in Scott's spiritual journey, he says, just a gradual awakening in his heart. "My faith is on a dimmer switch," he says. "It keeps getting brighter."

That conversation with Scott was just the first of several. As I walked through his shop, I held the cacao beans in my hand. I saw the simplicity and purity of his work, and I tasted the results. He was living under the same set of values that were driving my ravenous appetite for authenticity and community. He was making chocolate with all his heart, "as working for the Lord" (Colossians 3:23), and I was caught up in it. He loaded me down with samples of every kind of chocolate he made, and as I left, I vividly remembered the trail of M&Ms leaking from that Christmas package so long ago. As silly as it may sound, Scott's chocolate was all about Jesus. The purity, the friction, the heat, the tender care — everything about it was calling my heart back to a place I hadn't been in a while.

AN UNLIKELY STORY

Much of the path from seedpod to chocolate is covered over by history. We can only imagine what led to the first time a human being roasted some half-rotten seeds, ground them into a paste, and dared to eat the results. What kind of person does that? I like to imagine it was a creative, inquisitive, daring person who suspected there were mysteries just waiting to be discovered. Maybe it was someone who already had discovered other amazing secrets. It makes me wonder how many amazing discoveries I've passed up in my own life.

It's also astounding to think chocolate was being consumed for more than a thousand years before anyone thought to add sugar to it! The chocolate of pre-Columbian Mesoamerica was a bitter brew. I remember the time my grandmother was making one of her famous chocolate cakes and had a big pile of shaved Baker's Chocolate on her cutting board. She was called out of the kitchen for some reason, and she made sure to tell me not to sneak any of that chocolate. "I'd never know if you were to take a pinch. Please don't sneak any," she said. She didn't mention that the chocolate was unsweetened. Of course, I took a pinch. She'd practically instructed me to! She walked back into the kitchen just as I realized how bitter it was. I tried to hide my shock—and anger—but I now realize she saw right through me. There probably hadn't been any reason to leave the kitchen right then; she just wanted to have some fun watching a seven-year-old learn a lesson the hard way. All I know is that if I had been the one who'd first tasted cacao, there's no way I would have come back for more. I would have moved on to other rotten seeds. But something about chocolate kept people at the table for thousands of years before it got good.

Chocolate tells me some important things about God. He could have easily created it to be eaten in its raw state, like pineapples. But he didn't. In his sovereignty, goodness, and mercy, God created a way for us to participate with him in the creative process. He provided the raw materials—a scraggly tree that produces pods, each of which hold about forty slimy seeds, each of which in turn contains the exact genetic material needed to trigger the chemical changes necessary to make them edible. He also co-located naturally occurring yeast that is absolutely essential to the process of transforming the bitter cacao seeds into something wonderful.

The process of fermentation is a miracle in and of itself. It's no wonder people suspected magic. Unfermented cacao seeds have an astringent taste. In order to get the subtle, rich flavor we associate with high-quality chocolate, the beans must be fermented. To do this, the seeds are carefully pulled from the pod and placed in a special box called a sweatbox, where airborne wild yeast finds them and begins to feed on the sugars in the slime and, eventually, the beans. The yeast multiplies rapidly. The naturally occurring by-products of this fermentation are heat and alcohol (though the alcohol is much less than that created by fermenting grapes or grains). Workers rotate the seeds in carefully planned ways, making sure they are evenly exposed to the oxygen required by the fermenting yeast. As this process takes place, heat is given off. Temperatures inside the sweatboxes can easily reach over 120 degrees Fahrenheit. After fermentation is complete, the seeds are dried, packaged, and shipped to chocolatiers all over the world. If the seeds ferment for too long, they can spoil; if the fermentation isn't long enough, the seeds fail to chemically change and will require additives in order to taste like chocolate. The expert knows exactly how long it takes each batch of seeds to ferment and when to move them around in the box.

God gave us the ingredients for chocolate, and then he gave some of us creativity and some of us strong scientific minds. Chocolate does not exist outside of community, but because of it. No one person could have possibly figured out this process for making chocolate on his or her own.

God could have chosen to make chocolate a calorie-free food. He could have left out the explosive chemical reaction in the pleasure center of the human brain that makes us want to eat lots of it. He could have left out the caffeine or the acids. But he did none of those things. He gave us an opportunity to express our humanity through creativity, to work with others, to serve others, to enjoy ourselves, to cultivate discretion and moderation or take things too far. We can choose to add chemicals and preservatives to make chocolate cheaper or more consistent—even though it messes with chocolate's pure beauty. God lets us create alongside him, even when our creation defiles or cheapens his creation. Chocolate tells me something about the recklessness of his love. It reminds me of the abundant life he offers and of the responsibility we have to lovingly strive for the highest and truest manifestations of that abundance.

CHOCOLATE IS GOOD FOR YOU?

Could there be any scientific revelation more indicative of the truth that God is, in fact, good—and not some fuddy-duddy in the sky just itching to smack our hands—than the recent discovery that chocolate can actually be good for us? Now, don't set this book down and grab a candy bar from that secret stash of yours just yet. There are some strings attached.

A flurry of recent studies suggests a wide range of health benefits associated with high-quality chocolate. Cacao, it turns out, contains healthy fats and natural antioxidants called flavanols (flavonoid phytochemicals, to be sciency about it) that have been shown to have the following beneficial health properties:

- may decrease the risk of heart attack
- may decrease bad cholesterol and increase good cholesterol
- may contain anti-inflammatory properties
- may relieve stress (any woman could have told you that)
- may decrease blood pressure
- may increase insulin sensitivity (reduces risk of diabetes)
- may improve blood flow in the arteries (benefits cognition, eye health, relaxation)
- may help people feel full and eat less because of its high fiber content
- may aid in UV protection of the skin

These flavanols may also positively affect the function of neurotransmitters such as serotonin, which can affect sleep, mood, and stress. Chocolate also contains theobromine, an alkaloid similar to caffeine in some respects but generally believed to have positive health effects, including mild stimulation of the central nervous system, widening of the blood vessels, and relaxation of the vagus nerve, which may relieve persistent coughing.

The word *theobromine*, by the way, has nothing to do with the element bromine. In fact, the term comes from the Greek words *theo* (God) and *broma* (food). Thus, *theobromine* literally means "food of the gods."

Now for the not-so-good news: Not all chocolate is created equal. While some boutique chocolatiers, such as Olive & Sinclair, craft their product to contain high amounts of cacao and cacao butter and relatively lower amounts of sugar, most commercial chocolates are extremely high in sugars (including high fructose corn syrup) and dairy fats. Milk chocolate is usually low in actual cacao and therefore low in the critical flavanols that make chocolate beneficial. Chocolate is also a relatively high-calorie food. Eating too much milk chocolate can counteract the benefits by leading to weight gain from those extra calories and fat.

As is the case with many other foods, as well as with the ideas that shape our faith, there's the root thing itself, and then there's everything that gets added to or taken away from it. Sometimes it's good to strip things down to their essence, but there's a danger we'll lose something critical in the process. Cultural additives, personal prejudices, and unbiblical teachings may render our gospel more appealing, but that sweetness may come at the expense of the truth we seek. Too much cheap, corporate chocolate can hurt us in the same way beliefs tainted by artificial theological sweeteners corrupt our faith. But high-cacao dark chocolate, like pure gospel truth, is a joy and is actually *good* for us.

CHOCOLATY VERSUS CHOCOLATE:
PURITY MATTERS

If you see something labeled chocolaty, you should not consume it. There is a huge difference between chocolate and chocolaty. Chocolaty usually means a cheap, waxy product. It is a bad imitation of pure chocolate. I was once given a chocolaty rabbit in my Easter basket. I ate one bite of the poor beast's ears and felt sick. The ingredient list was full of unpronounceable chemicals, additives, artificial flavors, emulsifiers, and God knows what else. That mess was *not* chocolate. It was terrible.

And then there's carob. Carob has nothing to do with chocolate. It grows on bushes in the Middle East and is supposedly healthier than chocolate because it has no caffeine or theobromine. When I was a kid, carob was commonly used as an alternative to chocolate — the only problem being it was no healthier than chocolate and tasted nothing like chocolate. It was a lame alternative to the real thing. Carob made me mad. It was a poser. Just because something is brown does not make it chocolate.

And whoever made that chocolaty Easter Bunny tricked me once — but never, ever again. I read labels. I check ingredients. Life is too short for chocolaty when the real thing is available, and so much better than any imitation.

History is full of Christiany people, Christiany music, Christiany nations, and Christiany churches. They claim the name of Christ but seem uninterested or unwilling to submit to his authority or take his instructions seriously. They borrow the symbols but miss the meaning. Maybe like the carob people, they simply can't handle the idea that Christianity is rich, risky, sacrificial, dangerous, countercultural, hilarious, joyful, thrilling, lavish, and celebratory. Christiany preachers and teachers deify material blessings, place dangerous emphasis on the individual aspects of faith at the expense of the communal, and recklessly conflate the rhetoric and psychology of empire with the nature of the kingdom of God.

The thought that I might be living a Christiany life instead of a truly Christian life bothers me. As strange as it may sound, my reconnection with chocolate as something sacred has me thinking through the additives, preservatives, and artificial colors in my faith, which have cheapened it. In how many ways have I sacrificed purity for convenience? Is that why the fruit of my life often tastes so bland?

The goal of an artisan is to strip out the unhealthy and inauthentic so the true essence of a thing can shine through. The goal of modern manufacturing, however, is to dismantle the concept of absolutes and make everything relative to the perspective of each individual. "Who is to decide what true chocolate is anyway?" they seem to ask.

Ever since our hearts and minds were dislodged from the heart and mind of God in the garden of Eden, it seems we swing like a pendulum from extreme to extreme, missing true north as we pass from one pole to the other. The results of these swings are the many "isms" that describe humanity's relentless pursuit of meaning, peace, and belonging apart from

God. We see Jesus for a few moments at a time as we cycle between legalism and lawlessness, between death and love.

Industry was the engine of the Enlightenment. It pushed innovation and shaped values throughout the seventeenth and eighteenth centuries, moving society away from the muck and mire of superstition and myth. But not everyone was thrilled with the results. Artists searched for meaning in the machine, and philosophers questioned the dehumanizing effects of the factory. After a couple hundred years of enlightenment and industry, an aesthetic reaction took hold in the form of the romantics and then the modernists. The philosophy of modernism was originally used as a way to describe the changes taking place in the art world as creatives began to reject the underlying implications of both industry and reason. Modernism reveled in man's power to rearrange and control his reality. Impressionism sprang from modernist thought, as did an entire era of poetry, music, and even architecture. To the modernist mind, every problem had a solution waiting to be discovered. Humanity was being perfected, and a golden and glorious future was just around the corner.

Except it wasn't.

The term *postmodernism* first showed up in literature of the late nineteenth century but became well established decades later as the writings of Friedrich Nietzsche and other critics of modernism became wildly popular. If modernism was about building an ideal future or the perfect machine, then postmodernism, in all of its forms, was based on the concept of deconstruction. In the face of widespread suffering, corruption, unmet ideals, and the general failing of technology and reason to provide lasting internal peace, postmodernism called everything into question, including the very idea that anything could be truly known. Postmodernism questions the accessibility of objective truth and suggests that each person should define "meaning" on his or her own terms. Although this philosophical shift makes sense in the light of the limitations of modernism, when followed blindly it can encourage people to put anything in a pot and call it their own personal chocolate.

Contemporary spiritual sensitivities often either reject religious absolutes and elevate the individual to the highest position of authority or cling to the comfort and relative security of pharisaical legalism. While it can be good, healthy, and even exciting to rediscover the beauty of the gospel by disassembling some of the artifice of modern Christian culture, we must remember that underneath the flawed constructs of man lies a bedrock foundation of gospel truth. It is the Lord of *that* truth to whom we must run. Any truth that is subject to my sensitivities is useless, and any god that acquiesces to my sensibilities and preferences is certainly not worth serving.

The artisanal values inherent in these premodern, handcrafted, community-driven experiences confront some of the postmodern tenets of our era just as flagrantly as they challenge the factory values of industrialized Christianity. When it comes to chocolate, for instance, there are authentic ingredients, and there are artificial additives. There are more costly recipes that stick to real cacao grown and harvested with a sensitivity to the well-being of humans, and cheaper recipes that include flavor enhancers, preservatives, artificial colors, and tiny amounts of real cacao harvested cheaply by modern-day slaves. It's the same with our pursuit of God. If we stick to authentic ingredients, it will cost us more but ultimately will be healthier and more satisfying—and no one gets hurt.

Any craftsman will tell you that purity is essential. It is honored. It is valuable. The beauty of handmade works is that they avoid the additives that industrialism allows in the name of expedience or cost savings. Ingredients matter. Though a great deal of variety can be accomplished with additives, it is not up to me to decide I can add whatever I want to something and call it pure. When it comes to chocolate, there definitely *is* such a thing as absolute truth. It is not held captive by any -ism. I can no more add cheap alternatives to or subtract costly ingredients from the gospel I live than I can add brown food coloring to sugary wax and call it chocolate.

The good stuff—the authentic—in both chocolate and faith is available for those willing to seek it out. I hope I am.

Chapter 5

THE BEST COFFEE
I EVER HAD

I'll never forget my first cup of coffee. I was just twenty years old. Many of my friends, bandmates, and family members were already into coffee, but I hadn't yet developed a taste for it. Because of stomach problems when I was younger, coffee had been strictly off-limits (as was chocolate, now that I think about it). But by the time I turned twenty, my doctor gave me the green light to eat and drink normally. Considering how desperate my java-chugging friends were for coffee, however, I held it in about the same esteem as cigarettes, crystal meth, and Star Trek, which is to say I didn't esteem it at all. I figured there must be something powerfully attractive about it, and so it was best I kept my distance. Addiction terrified me.

But Michelle liked coffee, and I liked Michelle. I saw her walk through the door of our little church one Sunday morning and immediately made my way over to welcome her and her friends. After hearing her sing a "special music" song one Sunday, I invited her to sing with the worship team. After rehearsals, many of the team would hit Perkins Restaurant by the freeway. Michelle and I were usually the last ones there — her drinking coffee and me drinking soda water, talking about romantic woes and slowly falling in love. Well, for her it was slow, anyway. It was at the Cornerstone Festival in 1990 that we first kissed. Once we started dating, it was just a matter of weeks until we were engaged. We drove to St. Louis one weekend so I could meet her parents. I asked her to marry me on that trip. Less than two months later, she said yes, and I called her dad for his blessing. Yes, I called him. Not a good idea. We set a time to drive down to their house in St. Louis to talk it over.

To say I bungled the process of winning over her folks would be an understatement of magnificent proportions. After two days of small talk, we finally had The Conversation. "Kid," I distinctly remember him saying (though Michelle insists I have manufactured much of this dialogue in my imagination), "I don't like you. I don't even know you. I don't care whether you live or die. As far as I'm concerned, you're just the lucky SOB who caught my daughter on the rebound." Again, Michelle insists he said nothing close to this. But while he may not have said it with his mouth, it's what I heard. He did tell me, in no uncertain terms, that he was not in favor of our decision to get married, nor was he a fan of any kid who would ask for his daughter's hand after just a few weeks of dating. I believed he was pretty sure our church was a cult. The whole conversation was a nightmare. Now I endeavor to be just as terrifying to young men who want to court my daughter.

While I drove home that day, Michelle stayed behind for an extended visit. I figured I'd never see her again. It was clear to me that her father and the rest of her friends and family would spend the next week trying to undo the brainwashing I had obviously performed on her. I drove home in my black Hyundai Excel, tail between my legs and on the verge of tears. I cranked up a mix tape of heartbreak songs I kept handy at all times. It was pouring rain as I hit Springfield on Interstate 55. I pulled up behind a glass truck that was weaving in the wind. Massive windowpanes were banging against the rails they were strapped to, and a ladder looked like it might fall from the back door where it was mounted. As nervous as I was about driving in the downpour, I was even more nervous being behind that truck. I decided to pass it. I turned off the air-conditioning, and my car experienced the necessary burst of horsepower to pass the truck. Cruising right in front of the rig, however, was an Illinois state trooper. The speed limit had dropped ten miles per hour, but I'd missed the sign because of the storm and the truck. The officer pulled me over, looking extremely irritated to have to stand in the rain as he wrote me my first speeding ticket.

Just like that, I was an outlaw. My squeaky-clean self-image was forever tarnished. I was a speeder. I was bad. I was so rattled that I pulled off at the next rest stop to gather myself. There it was, in the lobby of the building—a coffee vending machine. *I'm just going to do it!* I said to myself, possibly aloud. *It's time for me to go dark. I'm a bad guy now. I live on the edge. I'm not safe at all. It's time to drink coffee!*

Now, little old ladies drank coffee after church every Sunday at St. Mark's. I'm not sure why this personal act felt so rebellious, but it did. I put in some quarters, selected Light, and then held down the Add Sugar and Add Lightener buttons with all my might. I noticed that the machine knew better than to call that stuff cream. What squirted into my cup was twelve ounces of hot beige liquid I was pretty sure was flammable. It tasted, culinarily and maybe theologically, like hell. *Perfect*, I said to myself. *This tastes as crappy as I feel.*

I nursed that cup all the way to the Dixie Truck Stop south of Bloomington. The cooler it got, the worse it tasted. I choked down about half of the cup and then got another at the truck stop. I hated the taste, but I forced it down anyway. In addition to embracing my new devil-may-care dark side, I figured if I ever did get to see Michelle again, I might as well develop a taste for coffee. Maybe that would be a point in my favor. My years of Mountain Dew abuse prevented any recognizable effects from the caffeine. That coffee was so bad that, after brushing my teeth a dozen times, I could still taste it.

Most people say it takes a while to develop a taste for coffee, but I was a quick learner. Michelle did come back to me after that week, and one night we went to a specialty coffee store at the mall. The salesman talked me into buying a relatively high-end coffee brewer, as well as a gold mesh filter and a grinder so I could buy whole beans. He explained the basics of specialty coffee and sold me a pound or two of beans. Within weeks of my first ignominious coffee experience, I became a complete coffee snob. I cultivated a taste for high-end java, and within a couple of months, I was drinking it black. Now I roast my own beans.

GOATHERDS, POPES, IMAMS, AND REVOLUTIONARIES

My obsessive side is most obvious when you consider my record collection and how I went crazy for coffee within weeks of my first cup. The same way I need to know the story behind any song, I needed to know the story behind coffee. Why are some beans worth so much more than others? Why does coffee from different areas taste so different, even though the species of coffee plants are identical? I've read books and sought out experts in order to piece together a biography of the revolutionary coffee bean.

Although its true origins are obscured by myth and legend, we know coffee first came from Ethiopia, probably around the thirteenth century. One legend tells of an Ethiopian goatherd named Kaldi who noticed that when his goats ate the red berries from a certain shrub, they began jumping around energetically. Kaldi tried the berries himself and felt the stimulating effects. He rushed to a local Islamic monk for guidance about his discovery. The monk objected to the berries and threw them into the fire. When they started roasting and giving off a pleasant smell, they were pulled from the coals and placed in hot water — and the first cup of coffee was brewed. While historians see this story as simply a myth, it is clear that coffee was first discovered in Muslim North Africa and was closely connected to spirituality from the very beginning.

Islamic, Roman Catholic, and Orthodox religious leaders

were suspicious of the stimulating effects of coffee at first, but by the late eighteenth century, those objections faded. Pope Clement is credited with officially sanctioning coffee in 1600 after a group of priests lobbied to brand it as satanic because of its Muslim roots. Legend has it that Clement responded to the request by saying "This devil's drink is so delicious ... we should cheat the devil by baptizing it." In eighteenth-century New England, coffeehouses became critical clearinghouses of news, gossip, political theorizing, and even sedition. With tea serving as a symbol of Great Britain's unjust treatment of the colonies, many American revolutionaries embraced coffee as part of their national identity.

Technological innovations associated with the Industrial Revolution brought the once exotic coffee bean to every kitchen in America. Coffee was transformed from an artisanal product with specific geographic and cultural roots into an anonymous brown powder—pre-ground or brewed and freeze-dried, then sold in metal cans or glass jars. Massive corporations, armed with factories, slave labor, and agricultural tech weaponry, took five hundred years of mystery, canned it, and made it common and cheap.

In the early 1970s, coffee's tide began to turn. A handful of advocates dreamed of recapturing some of the magic that had been lost. Specific flavor profiles associated with different regions were rediscovered, and for the first time in a long time, outliers could purchase whole bean coffee from Brazil, Colombia, Sumatra, Kenya, and other regions. Companies like Peet's and the original Seattle-based Starbucks began to redefine what good coffee could and should taste like. This movement has continued and has become typified by the cultural dominance of Starbucks. Millions of people now buy their coffee in roasted whole bean form, something unheard-of fifty years ago. There are also a host of new coffee innovators digging even deeper into the complexity of the mystical coffee beans.

In 2004, I took a monthlong trip to Central and South America helping The Evangelical Alliance Mission (TEAM) tell the stories of their various service projects in Latin America. I spent several days in Tegucigalpa, Honduras, as the guest of a businessman and church member who supported a wide range of local ministry projects. I mentioned my desire to see an actual rain forest, so one morning he took me to see some of his property. We hiked for a couple of hours before coming to a clearing in the woods. He picked some berries from a tree and asked if I knew what they were. When he removed the fleshy bit from the seeds, I could see the familiar shape of a coffee bean— though they were much larger and paler than I had expected. I put a handful in my pocket and then later into one of my bags. By the time I made it back to the States a week later, the beans had dried up and looked similar to the dried green coffee beans I buy today.

By the row of coffee trees, I met the local farmer my host employed to cultivate this small crop. She appeared to be in her eighties and lived in a stone cottage with open windows and doors. Wild dogs and chickens roamed freely. Shoeless children with obvious nutritional deficiencies emerged from the forest to see me up close. My host translated for me that the children had never seen a white person before — or a person over six feet tall, for that matter. After seeing this level of poverty and meeting coffee growers who seemed to be living on just a few dollars a month, I began wondering where the twelve dollars a pound I was paying for coffee went. That was when my host explained the function of middlemen and cartels. The injustice of it all was confusing, disheartening, and maddening.

Prior to that visit to Honduras, I had done similar work in Mexico's Baja Peninsula. There I spent several days with Steve Dresselhaus, a missionary who managed to seamlessly combine his love of scuba diving, kayaking, hiking, and other outdoor activities with his ministry work. Steve encouraged my deep love of all things Mexicana by exposing me to food, art, coffee, and people who melted my heart.

One evening, after a long day working at a pop-up medical mission in Ciudad Constitución, a few hours' drive from La Paz, we stopped in a "town" called San Hilario. I actually don't remember anything that could be described as town-like. In fact, there weren't even roads. Somehow, Steve knew how to get through the rocky desert trails in his Econoline van, following a sort of path I couldn't distinguish within the desert landscape. He was excited to show us their latest church plant and to introduce me to a couple of the founding families.

When we finally came to a stop, we were a short walk from a tiny hut made from stones, cinder blocks, plastic sheeting, and corrugated metal. A blue tarp had been suspended on poles over a makeshift table and chairs outside of the hut to create a sort of courtyard. The small homestead belonged to an older couple who had been instrumental in starting the new church. Gregorio was thin, leathery, white-headed, and strong. Though he spoke no English, he shook my hand and greeted me with one of the brightest smiles I've ever seen. Shaking his hand felt like grabbing a warm stone. His hands were so calloused they did not feel human. Steve said he was a cowboy for a local rancher.

A short hike brought us to a concrete slab. "Here's the church," Steve beamed. "The slab?" I asked. "Yes sir," he replied, still grinning like a proud papa. "We can set up a tent to provide shade, and the flat surface allows us to set up chairs. It's not much, but everyone is pretty excited about it." Members of Steve's church in La Paz had raised the necessary funds for the concrete and had come out to lay this foundation. I had often heard it said, and had even said it myself, that church isn't about a building. Never had that reality been more apparent to me than at that moment.

With the afternoon shadows lengthening, Steve was concerned we make our way out of the desert before it got too dark. Our hosts insisted on providing refreshments before we left. They prepared coffee by placing a small percolator filled with water directly in the flames of a wood-burning fire inside their hut. Gregorio reached into the fire with his bare hands to rearrange the burning logs so the coffeepot would fit. He threw a handful of coffee grounds into the pot and let it boil. It was by far the most primitive place I had visited at that point in my life. The sun was setting over the desert landscape as the scent of the coffee began to waft through the hut. The smoke in the room was burning my eyes and throat, so we retreated to the "courtyard" and took our seats under the tarp. There on the table sat three dainty porcelain cups. When the coffee was ready, our hostess poured it, and I took a sip. I had never tasted coffee that good.

It's been more than ten years, and I still remember it as being one of the best cups of coffee I've ever had. It was served black, with a bit of Mexican brown sugar to sweeten it. I sat at that table with our hosts and my travel companions and shared stories about our journey thus far. The coffee was surprisingly mellow and smooth, with no bitterness or charred flavors. I've come to realize, though, that my love of that coffee had more to do with the overall experience than what was actually in the cup. Language, ethnic, and cultural barriers stole nothing from the authentic fellowship we experienced. The coffee wasn't central to the moment; the people were. But I remember the flavor as though I've just finished sipping it.

ESCAPING THE DARK SIDE

While Starbucks has done wonderful things to advance the appreciation of coffee over the last couple of decades, one of the more unfortunate repercussions of its legacy is the ubiquity of chronically overroasted beans. For an entire generation of coffee drinkers, "good coffee" means "dark coffee." For many years, I was no exception. There was a certain acrid taste we all associated with high-end roasts. It turns out, though, that the beans were pretty much just burned. The successors of Peet's and Starbucks, known as Third Wave Coffee roasters, are pushing back on the notion that dark coffee means good coffee and discovering wonderful flavors that are only noticeable in lighter roasts. To its credit, Starbucks is moving to the lighter end of the spectrum as well.

The process of roasting chemically changes a coffee bean. High heat creates a Maillard reaction between the amino acids and sugars in the bean. This is the same process that creates a crust on bread. But just like bread, if the process continues for too long or if the temperature is too high or too low, the results can be disastrous. If the beans are underroasted, they taste grassy and terrible, and they're too hard to grind. If roasted for too long, they will burn. If the temperature is too high, they roast too quickly; if the temperature is too low, they merely bake. The challenge is to expose the beans to the proper temperature for the right amount of time, then cool them quickly to stop the process.

Different types of beans from different locations reveal different flavors at different roasting points. Lighter roasts produce brighter notes and fruity aromas, while darker roasts produce richer, chocolaty, or even wine-like notes.

As with toast, though, people's tastes vary. Some people like their toast very light, while others like it charred. The simple scientific fact is that the longer something is roasted, the more we taste the *roast* as opposed to the thing itself—and this is definitely true of coffee.

The mistake of overroasting beans to get strong coffee is one of the great culinary crimes of the era, and thousands of well-meaning coffee snobs are dying to set the record straight. The strength of coffee has to do with the ratio of coffee to water. Light roast coffee can be very strong, and dark roast coffee can be very weak. The means of brewing also contributes to the flavor. The temperature of the water, the particle size of the ground coffee, the amount of time the coffee is exposed to the water, and the filtering mechanism all shape the strength and flavor of the final cup. A basic cup of coffee can be brewed with a drip brewer, a pour-over system (my favorite is the Chemex), a French press, or even an espresso machine. Each method will produce a different level of flavor from the same coffee.

Experimenting with roasting, grinding, and brewing provides nearly infinite flavor possibilities. Done properly, the resulting cup can be rich, smooth, and even sweet. More importantly, though, a good cup of coffee doesn't need cream and sugar! Cream is to coffee what milk is to chocolate. It dilutes the flavor. Cream and sugar mask the underlying flavor of the beans. When coffee is bad or even just average, cream and sugar can be helpful. But the best coffee doesn't need either. In fact, don't be surprised when a coffee purist insists you try his or her coffee black before adding pollutants.

The principles are the same with our faith. Are we adding cream and sugar in the form of shallow and unbiblical adjuncts to mask the astringent taste of a poorly constructed gospel? Are we missing the intrinsic flavors of a life in the Spirit by overroasting our dogma in the fire of our fears and judgmental fervor? Is our relationship with God and his people something we approach with a utilitarian agenda or an aesthetic one?

With care, precision, and coaching, we can choose to invest the effort, coax a deeply satisfying, and rich spiritual experience from the ingredients given to us by God. The question remains: Do we just *need* a cup of coffee or are we ready for something transcendent?

A COFFEE GURU CALLS

The path of coffee from tree to cup is relatively simple. The cherries, or beans, ripen about nine months after their flowers are pollinated. They are harvested by hand or, in some cases, by machine. The seeds are removed from the fleshy part and dried. They are separated by size, then manicured for defects, and packaged to be shipped to a roaster or distributor. Once dried, the beans can be stored for up to a year, until the next harvest. They will slowly degrade over that time, making blends the easiest way to maintain quality consistency. After roasting, however, staling moves quickly; large amounts of carbon dioxide are released, and the volatile oils that give the coffee its flavor begin to escape. That's why roasted coffee beans smell so good when they are fresh. They are actively "gassing off" their essence. Once the roasted beans are ground and exposed to the air, the staling process accelerates significantly. Thus, the shorter the time between roasting, grinding, and brewing, the more flavor and aroma will be imparted to the brewed coffee. Many commercial coffees linger for months or more after roasting. The coffee I brew at home, however, never lasts for more than a few days. I get a lot of credit for being a great roaster, when really it's that my coffee is fresher than anything you can buy commercially.

The main factors that determine the flavor of coffee are the species of bean (Arabica or Robusta); the variety of Arabica; environmental conditions, such as soil and climate (the *terroir*) of the farm it was grown on; the craftsmanship of the farmer and of the processor; the packaging and transportation; the way it was roasted (called the "roast profile"), which is different for every bean; the brew method; and the quality, temperature, and ratio of the water used to brew it. Even slight variations in any of these factors can significantly change the final product. Great care, attention to detail, and ongoing review are required to produce real quality.

Over the years, as I've sought wisdom from coffee experts and become more familiar with the high-end coffee experience, one name has come up over and over. If I really wanted to hear from an expert, I was told, I needed to talk to George Howell. To my surprise, an email to his website caught his attention, and one morning he gave me a call.

George is, at the age of seventy, internationally famous as one of the most significant personalities in the decommodification of coffee. To the most refined coffee palates in the world, he is a guru. In 1974 in the Boston area, he opened Coffee Connection, one of the most acclaimed coffee shops in the United States. Over the next twenty years, his business expanded to twenty-four cafes. Coffee Connection came to source its beans from individual farmers around the world, and George became one of the foremost experts in coffee cupping (tasting) and light roasting. His team created the original Frappuccino, which he sold along with his business to Starbucks in 1994.

In 1997, George was invited by the International Trade Centre of the United Nations to be a quality consultant for Brazil's coffee industry. "The project," he explains, "was originally called the Gourmet Project and was established by the International Coffee Organization in London. I flew several times a year, crisscrossing Brazil—which is a huge place—and learning coffee in a whole new way." George's job was to improve the quality and reputation of Brazilian coffee by helping craft-motivated farmers implement better methods and technologies related to growing, harvesting, preparing, and shipping their beans, thus opening the possibility of freeing them from the commodity market.

The vast majority of coffee grown worldwide is harvested

by individual farmers who sell their crops to central buyers. These buyers combine the beans into one big pile and pay the growers based on a worldwide commodity price. Any unique flavor notes of beans from a particular farm are lost in the region's blend. Because the price of any commodity is based on international supply and demand, the system allows no room for one farmer to invest more in their employees, to reject environmentally damaging pesticides, or to do anything else to increase costs. There is just no incentive.

Although the name "Cup of Excellence" wasn't George's idea, the concept behind the project certainly was. With the support of the Specialty Coffee Association of America (SCAA) and the Gourmet Project in Brazil, and blessed with a brilliant team of Brazilian professionals on the ground, George cocreated with marketing specialist Susie Spindler an event that connected the best coffee growers with the most serious international buyers and roasters. The farmers submitted green samples of their best current lot, which were then light-roasted to provide the cleanest, clearest examples of each farm's unique *terroir*. The roasters and buyers then did a blind-taste cupping and rated each one, over and over again during many days. The lots were then ranked and auctioned online to buyers. "Because of my reputation," George says, "I was able to get key players in the industry to come. Ted Lingle, the executive director of the SCAA, and Jim Reynolds, the buyer from Peet's, were there, as were many prominent buyers from Europe and Japan." George's efforts worked. The prices on the winning lots were about 35 percent higher than the market price would have been.

Although I'm enough of a coffee freak to find all of these nuances fascinating, there's an undercurrent that is pulling me through this point in our conversation. You're probably wondering how the farming techniques of Central Americans relate to the gospel Jesus brought. The story of the Cup of Excellence is a rescue tale. By pulling individual farms out of the commodity process, the individual flavors that make their crops unique can be appreciated. George and his compatriots are rescuing coffee from the great averaging process that has kept growers chained for hundreds of years. Coffee beans don't need chemical flavors sprayed on them after roasting. A good, light roast and a nice, clean brew allow even amateur tasters to pick up the subtle flavors and essences that make coffee beans unique.

The Cup of Excellence changed everything for specialty coffee consumers and producers. The winning farmers earned a better price than ever before—certainly enough to incentivize them to take steps to continue improving the quality of their crops—and the buyers were able to secure a higher quality of coffee with all the unique flavors intact. By helping these small to medium-sized farms segregate their beans in terms of quality—with lower grade beans selling for a lower price to one market, and higher quality beans being recognized and valued appropriately—farmers were able to see significant increases in their profits.

I wonder what would happen to the value of our faith if we could rescue it from the process of commodification. If a life spent in pursuit of Christ could be recognized as a radical and selfless, counterintuitive adventure instead of a carefully packaged and lifeless script, would seekers find something worth following? Might new flavors—notes that had been there all along but had been lost in the pile—reemerge? Might the aroma of such a faith draw in people who aren't the least bit interested in the kind of factory faith that has been cleverly marketed to them by churches obsessed with growth?

If you had been at my house during Christmastime 2013, you could have had a cup of coffee grown by the Villatoro family in the Huehuetenango region of Guatemala. This crop, called Finca Villaure, was an award winner in the 2013 Cup of Excellence competition. I was able to get a few pounds to roast at home. I paid $15.49 per pound, which is about three times higher than many of the green beans I buy but still cheaper than any of the higher quality roasted beans you can purchase at Starbucks or the grocery store. At a roast somewhere between light and medium, this coffee is amazing. I could detect subtle notes of berry and dark chocolate. I remember rolling my eyes when people with more sophisticated palates would talk about "picking up notes of ..." and then list a seemingly bizarre combination of references. I know that someone with a taste for Caramel Macchiatos might recoil at the idea of thoughtfully sipping black coffee, but in a relatively short amount of time, I've learned to pick up these notes, and my enjoyment of coffee has increased exponentially. I promise that a well-grown, well-roasted, well-ground, and well-brewed cup of coffee can be so much more than the cream and sugar delivery vehicle I first tried at the Dixie Truck Stop.

BEYOND FAIR TRADE

There have always been those who seek out the highest quality examples of coffee—or chocolate or wine or art—because they can afford the best and have developed a taste for it. I'm not one of those people. I've never been wealthy by American standards. For me and many of my friends who are becoming interested in economic factors such as living wages and environmental preservation, there is more rolled into the value of a thing than its price. Financially challenged as we may be, it's an easy choice to support Scott Witherow and the Villatoros, and others like them, even if it costs more. I had always been led to believe that fair trade was about assuring consumers that manufacturers were paying fair wages to their workers. Hearing the stories of farmers at the Cup of Excellence caused me to suspect I'd been had.

"How is this kind of direct, relationship-based trade different from what we know as fair trade?" I asked George Howell. "It seems the current generation is working a lot more than pure aesthetics into their perception of a thing's value."

"Yes," George responded, "many young people are very idealistic. But early on, the quality of Fair Trade Certified or organic coffee just wasn't there. While the objectives seemed great, the product was often mediocre at best. The quality-price incentive didn't really function beyond delivering whatever might be acceptable in a commodity sense."

The problem, it turned out, was that the cost associated with getting a crop certified as organic was prohibitively expensive for poor farmers. Many who treat their employees fairly and follow organic guidelines couldn't get the certification because they couldn't afford it. When too many farmers went organic in certain areas, competition lowered prices, which in turn lowered quality standards.

Ethical certifications, in fact, are just one more way we busy consumers can choose to abdicate our personal responsibility to be good neighbors. We're too busy or simply don't have access to connect personally with the farmer who grows the coffee beans we purchase or the vegetables we eat or the cows providing the beef we grill. So we do the modern industrialist thing: we hire out our ethics to panels of people who are paid quite handsomely to do our discerning for us. It's convenient. It's expedient. It brands us as concerned people. It makes us feel good about ourselves or at least better about our conspicuous consumption, but is it true? And do we really want to know?

"We're bombarded with all these choices and controversies," George continues. "We want nothing more than to just park our conscience on the shelf somewhere." For him and many others, the responsibility to do more than this means developing personal relationships with the farmers who produce what we eat and drink. George understands that part of his job is to do the discerning for the busy consumer, though, and to do it well. It's a job he takes very seriously.

"Relationship coffee has it limits too," he admits. "It's based on contracts or agreements that say, 'I'm going to pay you this price for this year or for the next three years or five years.' It still has a somewhat paternalistic structure to it. The ultimate ethical goal is that the farmer can stand on his own two feet. But that requires the roaster to recognize he is in competition with other buyers for the very farm he has a relationship with. That's not a popular subject for a lot of roasters because it is extremely discomforting." George cites the example of vintners who successfully untethered themselves from the commodity pricing of grapes in the nineteenth century. "Suddenly an especially good vintage would be worth considerably more than a typical wine. This is the same approach we used with the Cup of Excellence for coffee."

So today George must continue to navigate and coordinate the aesthetic, scientific, and economic issues related to coffee. He and a growing network of mostly younger generation coffee roasters are helping to pull farmers out of the trap of anonymity and give them a name. As a result, their craft — the growing of coffee — becomes much more valuable. Again, the percentage is tiny, but the results are influential and growing.

George's greatest concern about the future of specialty coffee is the devastating effect changing weather patterns are having on coffee crops. "Right now," he says, "we're seeing a fungus that was limited to an altitude of three thousand feet suddenly jump to six thousand feet and hit farmers who were previously immune because of the weather patterns. There were always changes, but not like now." While massive agribusiness ventures can genetically modify their crops to be disease resistant, many boutique growers have far less recourse. Additionally, as a coffee plant has traditionally been bred strictly for heartiness, it can easily lose more of its subtle flavor characteristics. It's not hard to imagine a future with one type of boring, cheap, genetically modified coffee—a world in which the unique notes are muted by the din of agricultural industrialism—unless quality farm coffees receive the attention George Howell and a growing number of other roasters believe they deserve.

George's influence can be found in all aspects of the Third Wave Coffee renaissance. Craft roasters, baristas, shop owners, and boutique distributors have intentionally moved the clock backward on coffee, applying modern scientific understanding, hipster style, the romance of yesteryear, and hyperlocal sensitivities to the craft of coffee but running the entire process through a decidedly nonindustrial filter. Third Wavers are also weaving information about harvesting practices, pesticides, employee treatment, irrigation techniques, and other human and environmental factors into the value of the final product. The age-old values of industrial commerce are being upended as these artists and their customers intentionally choose to pay more for coffee that not only tastes better but also feels better. Moral issues are woven into both the cost and the appreciation of the final cup.

Again, all of this makes me think of what we've done to the gospel. What have we lost in our pursuit of scale and acceptance? Has the megachurch era been like the Starbucks era? Despite its fall from grace with the hipsters and coffee aficionados, Starbucks has done a lot to change how people experience and value coffee. Similarly, millions of people have benefited from the cultural relevance and approachability of the evangelical church over the last few decades. Maybe it's just that some of us have come to a new place where we need something more personal, authentic, and simple. This doesn't necessarily mean we swear off "Big Church" — or Starbucks, for that matter. Maybe we just add something more handcrafted into the mix. For us, it's meant intentionally connecting in a meaningful and consistent way with a smaller number of people. It's about going deeper instead of wider. While gathering with a large number of fellow pilgrims is exciting, time spent face-to-face with the members of our small group is essential. We pray for each other. We bear each other's burdens and celebrate each other's victories. We pursue God together as a group. We drink great coffee.

NEVER WASH THE POT

My personal path into the world of specialty coffee got a major boost a couple of years ago, thanks to my friend Tommy Ogle. Tommy was a banjo-playing, string-band-loving product of the '60s Jesus Movement. We met at a Cornerstone Festival. He sat in with my band, The Wayside, several times and invited me to his home church in Paris, Tennessee, to sing and teach. Tommy had a beard down to his belly, a floppy old hat, and the sort of gentle humor that put everyone at ease. He was a protohipster — the real deal.

Tommy and his wife, Rebecca, visited our home in Nashville shortly after we made the move south from Chicago.

Actually, they came over many times, never minding the two-hour drive. One weekend, they helped us paint our family room, the space we intended to use for our home group meetings. We heard stories about his youth, about how he and Rebecca met and how he came to faith, and about some of the great concerts he had seen. And we went through a lot of coffee. Tommy loved coffee.

At one point during their visit, as I was in the kitchen cleaning up, I grabbed the coffeepot to wash it. Tommy stopped me cold. "You should never wash a coffeepot or coffee cup with soap," he insisted gently. "It messes up the flavor." Once a cup had been washed with soap, Tommy figured it was permanently ruined. I'm not sure I completely agree, but to this day, every time I wash a coffee cup, I hear him chide me.

Tommy was diagnosed with cancer a few years back. He put up a good fight, but once it was clear it was only a matter of time before he would lose his battle, he invited all of his friends to a musical celebration in Paris, Tennessee. He called to see if Michelle and I would sing a few songs. "I figure it's kind of silly to wait until I'm gone," he said. "I can't enjoy all the music then." Of course we went. The night was amazing. Michelle and I were flat-out schooled in string band music.

Tommy arranged for us to stay with his friend Dan Knowles after the celebration. "I've been wanting you to meet Dan for years," he said. "I think you two are kinda cut from the same cloth." Dan, it turns out, is one of the most respected banjo builders and old-time string band performers in the region. He and Tommy had been friends for a long time and had even done some recording together. Tommy built gourd banjos in Dan's shop. "Make sure to try his coffee," he said. "He makes some good coffee, for sure." The morning after the event, I woke up early and found Dan in his kitchen. I drank a cup of his coffee. It was excellent. It reminded me of camping. He offered me another cup, but I said I was limiting my caffeine intake. "This stuff's decaf," he said with a wink. I was floored. It didn't taste like decaf at all. He told me it tasted so good because he roasted it himself. I was floored again.

I told Dan I had been interested in coffee roasting for years and had done a lot of research but couldn't spare the funds to buy a roaster. Dan smiled at me and said, "You can start roasting coffee for about twenty-five bucks." *Sure*, I thought. *This guy can make a banjo out of an old pumpkin; he's probably some kind of hillbilly MacGyver.* He said, "Come here; I'll show you. Grab your coat."

We went to Dan's front porch, where he produced a Wagner heat gun — the kind used for stripping paint — and an old metal pot. He poured about a cup of green coffee beans into the pot, put on some gloves, turned on the heat gun (picture a small hair dryer that cranks out 800 degrees of heat), and started warming up the beans. He explained that the outer layer of a bean would slough off once it expanded a bit. The resulting chaff would start to float out of the pot. He said the beans would start to smoke once they got to a certain point — and then we'd hear a cracking sound. "That's called the first crack," he explained. "You can either stop right there or keep going to the second crack." Dan let me roast a batch, instructing me to shake the pot with my left hand to keep the beans moving and to aim the heat gun in just the right way to get the right roast going. "Too close, and the beans burn," he said. "Too far, and they bake." When they were done, I poured them on a plate to let them cool. He said to let them rest a bit, then grind them and brew them the next day. He even gave me a small portion of beans to take home to roast on my own, and he pointed me to the website for Burman Coffee in Wisconsin, where he orders his beans.

I was hooked. The whole thing was so simple, and yet so precise. When I saw Tommy, I told him what Dan had taught me. "Good," Tommy said. "I had a feeling he'd get you in some trouble." Boy had he ever. Before the next week was over, I had purchased a heat gun of my own, found an old pot at Goodwill, and was out back roasting my own coffee. Clouds of smoke and a smell like burnt toast billowed from behind our house several times a week for the next year. I got pretty good at it and had fun experimenting with beans from all over the world. Our home group noticed the improved quality of the house coffee. I had found a new focus for my coffee passion that was both fun and saved me money. The following Christmas, Michelle and the kids got me a small roasting machine. I haven't purchased roasted coffee since. I've found my favorite beans and regularly try new ones.

We lost Tommy not long after that night of music. Michelle and I sang the old Louvin Brothers' song "The Christian Life" at his memorial. The memory of his sweet spirit seems to pervade my basement office where the roasting happens now. It always smells a little smoky. I keep an old banjo hanging over my writing desk, and an even older banjo uke that Tommy refurbished for me is nearby. Sometimes I forget he's gone.

COST, WORTH, VALUE, COFFEE, AND A DESK

Coffee is my daily reminder that there is a major difference between cost and value. The industrial creed reinforces the idea that cheap is better and profit is king. While frugality is a positive habit to foster and it's good to save money when you can, when industrialism helps you save cash by making things cheaper, it's usually so you can and will buy more junk. The spiritual implications are profound. Cheap is often just cheap.

Conversely, just because something costs more doesn't mean it's better. Once we become fully assimilated into the industrial world's value system, we can easily be manipulated to ascribe value to a thing based solely on its cost or profit potential. Therefore, Starbucks coffee must be better than McDonald's coffee because it's twice as expensive. I once met an older man at the YMCA who complained that before all the youngsters started moving into East Nashville, you could get a cup of coffee for fifty cents. "Who in the world would pay five dollars for a cup of coffee?" he asked. I kept my mouth shut.

Capitalism may be the most effective and powerful economic force in this fallen world, but it never saved anyone's soul. What was that cup of coffee in the Mexican desert worth to me? In dollars and cents, probably not very much.

The experience, though, was priceless. When economic principles shape the way we value human beings and form relationships, we rob ourselves, and our neighbors, of the sacredness of our humanity. How often do we contribute to the exploitation of others by pursuing only our own personal gain? We turn community into a marketplace.

You can run anything through a formula to calculate what it's really worth. Start with the cost, and make sure to factor in as many costs as you can as opposed to just the obvious ones. What does it cost you in dollars? In time? In attention? What does it cost the environment? Your community? Your neighbor? Then consider the value. What does the thing accomplish? How does it make life better for you? How does it make life better for your neighbor? How does it affect your connection to others, to creation, to God? A fast-food cheeseburger might not cost much money—but it does cost me something in terms of health. It does cost the environment something.

The same goes for cheap coffee, cheap chocolate, and cheap bread.

However, there are times when a thing seems to cost much more in terms of dollars, time, or effort but yields a value that is much greater. The worth of such a thing might, in fact, turn out to be quite significant. Even if we're talking about a cheeseburger. Or a piece of furniture.

My friend Chris Barber is a master with wood. Chris makes furniture—desks, tables, chairs, beds, cabinets—that belongs in museums. He is truly an artist. I can't afford his stuff, but if this book does really well, don't be surprised to hear that I've invested in a Chris Barber desk or chair. I don't even want to think about the cheap pressboard furniture I've bought and eventually thrown away over the last twenty-five years. Chris's work never gets thrown away. I saw him at church the other day—one of those moments that made me glad to be a part of a larger community in addition to our small group—and I was reminded of a Wendell Berry quote my farmer friend Bill Guerrant shared with me: "Furniture should have the durability of wood, not glue."

I shared that with Chris as we filled our coffee cups in the back of the sanctuary. He lit right up. "Many of the things that make furniture stronger than the glue," he said, "aren't necessarily supercomplex things but things that are opposed to mass production. In an assembly line, you can bolt things on and put enough glue on so it will stay together for a while, but that's it. There are a lot of things you can do with craftsmanship that you just can't do quickly. It's not elaborate," he adds. "It's just skillful, and it can't be done in mass production."

Chris mentioned one particular technique he hadn't yet tried but knew was remarkably strong. "These old-school guys—they're making something like a Windsor chair, and they start with green lumber," he said. "Most builders use kiln-dried and prepared wood, but these guys make the chair with wet wood and put the joint in hot sand to allow the tenons to contract, and then they join the parts together. When the temperature goes back to normal, the wood expands, and that joint won't fail."

Chris is a master. While I could probably find a table at Target or IKEA for five hundred dollars, to have Chris make me a table from scratch might cost maybe five thousand dollars. People who know quality are lining up to work with him. He works with each client for several hours to understand exactly what they want. He hears their stories. He studies their living space. He explores materials. By the time he finishes a piece, he has spent exponentially more hours on it and has used finer and more durable materials than any mass-produced furniture brand. "Anything that is crafted," he says, "is the result of a partnership between the maker and the consumer. These things meet a simple need but are also artistic." Chris's furniture meets a physical need and a spiritual or soul need. "IKEA is a very successful business," he says, "because they meet both of those things in the short term. They have good design, and their products are functional for a time, but they use cheap materials that won't last. If you want a table, then a board and a couple of two-by-fours will get the job done, or something from Target or IKEA will work. But if I make a table and tell someone it's going to cost five thousand dollars, they might say, 'It's just a table!' They don't have any frame of reference for something that is handmade like this."

But some people do. And that's enough.

Chris gets the kind of creative satisfaction from his work you would expect in a songwriter, sculptor, or poet. "It sounds weird, but it's almost like jazz," he says. "You get music; you hear the twelve notes, and you think, *Yeah, I get this. Cool.* Then you hear jazz, and you're like, *This is something totally different!* It's the same in some ways, but it's outside the bounds of what is reasonable. That's what this kind of woodworking feels like."

It's like everything else, really. Good furniture costs more but lasts longer and looks better. Carefully grown, harvested, roasted, ground, and brewed coffee costs more than the factory stuff, but boy, does it taste better. A painting costs more than a print or the same image that's available online for free. It takes more time to find good music to listen to than it does to just go with the cultural flow and listen to whatever is on the radio or watch whatever is showing at the local cinema. Vinyl LPs cost more than CDs. It takes time to cultivate a few close, intimate relationships with people as opposed to just shaking the hands of a few dozen acquaintances on a Sunday morning. But sometimes—actually most of the time—the carefully crafted is worth far more to us than what it costs. It adds real value to our lives, not just a quick fix. It stays with us. It satisfies us. It inspires us.

Something as simple as coffee can reveal much about how we assign value, but the implications run deeper than what is in our cups. The industrial temptation to go for the cheapest option, to ignore the ethical implications of our consumption, or to choose not to refine our palates in order to recognize excellence and purity when we taste it is an unfortunate missed opportunity at best. We risk drowning out the still, small voice of God when we succumb to the noise of the marketplace and let it carry us away.

If my experience with the gospel had been like that first cup of rest stop coffee, I might never have returned. I fear this is true for many who are disconnected from God's people. In a moment of need or nostalgia, they may have crossed the threshold of a church building, only to encounter the astringent, acrid taste of vending machine community. Maybe they poured in copious amounts of sugar and lightener to make it more palatable. This could have come in the form of surface-level teaching, feel-good worship, or virtual community. That kind of commodification might fill the belly cheaply for a time, but it won't nourish the soul in the long term.

Community isn't cheap, and living as a member of the body of Christ is not easy. But the rewards that come from cultivating a taste for authentic community and a deeper faith are more than worth the cost. The more I dive into the messy process of cultivating deep and sustained relationships based on the timeless mystery of the gospel, the more rich and rewarding my spiritual journey becomes. When my neighbors catch a whiff of God's presence in my life, I sure hope it smells like a cup of freshly roasted, recently ground, home-brewed coffee and not like the nightmare sludge that came out of that machine on the side of Interstate 55 all those years ago.

Chapter 6

CIVILIZATION, REFORMATION, DISCERNMENT, AND BEER

*M*y mother's parents' house in Lombard, Illinois, was always ground zero for my entire extended family and a constantly growing network of adoptees who had been grafted into it. One holiday, my uncle Jerry said something that forced me to realize I was not nearly as together as I liked to think. I was about nineteen and had already been living in my own apartment for a while. I had opened up True Tunes and was actively involved in two different churches. I was feeling pretty much on top of the world and was excited to see everyone at my grandparents' house—the place I simply called 412 (its street address). I think I may have even had a new tape from my band to share. Jerry, whom I hadn't seen in quite some time, saw me coming toward the house and met me at the door with a huge smile and a big hug. "Johnny!" he exclaimed, "My God, you are the spitting image of your old man!"

I freaked out.

In the span of one second, I went from being happy, excited, and optimistic into a sort of psycho-emotional panic attack. I turned and ran—not even back to my car. I just bolted down the street toward the park. Eventually, my sprint turned into a walk, and I meandered around the neighborhood for more than an hour. I was embarrassed and confused at my own reaction. I tried unsuccessfully to hold back tears. I strongly considered sneaking back to my car and leaving. I knew that every single soul in that house— especially my uncle—loved me unconditionally and would not deliberately do or say anything to make me feel anything less than precious to them. The fear that I was doomed to become like my father, though, was palpable. It was so terrifying that for an hour or so it blocked out the light. Fortunately, though, I knew I couldn't just leave. I decided to go back, make up some story about suddenly feeling sick, and then say my good-byes.

I walked back into the house, and no one reacted unusually. I got the normal hugs and welcomes and offers of food. I thought maybe no one had noticed my little episode, but I realized later that they just knew it was best not to make a big deal out of it. I started to feel better. Slowly my true emotions started to align with the pleasantries coming out of my mouth. Within a few minutes, Uncle Jerry came back over to give me another big hug. "I'm sorry," he said quietly, so only I could hear. "I wasn't thinking about how that would make you feel. Your father had some great qualities," he added. "I actually got along with him really well, but I never saw the ugly side. He was bright and funny and smart—and you are too." I weakly apologized for freaking out and said I honestly had no idea what my panic was about. "Don't worry about it," he said with a huge smile. "We all have stuff to deal with." Except he didn't use the word *stuff*.

When I was a kid, I was terrified of beer. Actually, for most of my life I was scared of alcohol in general. At some point, I heard that addiction was hereditary. *If you have the gene, you're going to become an alcoholic the first time it passes your lips.* That was the sentiment, and it scared the crap out of me. What little I knew of my genetics didn't help. My biological father and several of his brothers were alcoholics. The disease lingered on my mother's side as well—plaguing my uncle Jerry. When I was a kid, alcoholism was the monster under my bed, waiting to devour me.

I steered clear of alcohol during my teen years. Part of my spiritual euphoria was my absolute refusal to partake in any mind-altering substances. I worried about those who did. Occasionally during high school, I was invited to deejay a party. I went, but I was the guy who hid the car keys of kids who had been drinking. I lectured my friends about the dangers of alcohol. I was an anti-drinking zealot.

Even my Grandpa Holton's rock-solid example of moderation, sobriety, and self-discipline was not enough to adequately counter my fear. In my head, I knew that not everyone who drank would become an alcoholic, but emotionally, I didn't believe it. My grandfather made wine when I was a kid. Once, he let my brother and me smash the grapes with our bare feet, which was pretty cool. I sometimes helped him with the wine-making equipment. There was something about the whole process that seemed sacred and scary, the same way God is sacred and scary. Grandpa told us about the science behind fermentation, and it felt holy to me. I associated wine with church and celebrations, but the alcohol in it was what filled my life with fear. I remember Grandpa showing me a bottle of rhubarb wine he had bottled when I was a baby. "Maybe we'll open this one and taste it when you turn twenty-one," he said. Even though that day was about fourteen years away at that point, I was terrified. Maybe that very rhubarb wine would turn me into an alcoholic.

My fear of addiction, I now realize, was a significant driver of my personality throughout my teen years and into my twenties. I also now realize my fear was about more than alcoholism; I was afraid of becoming anything like my father. Even after he was gone from our lives, he terrified me. I couldn't stand the fact that I came from him. My hatred for him permeated my sense of self. I spiritualized it, of course. I found some Bible verses about not being drunk but being filled with the Spirit (Ephesians 5:18) and about wine being a mocker and beer a brawler (Proverbs 20:1). I turned my fear into legalism and whitewashed it with a bucketful of devotion. My biological father was a monster—and the best I would ever be in this life, I feared, was a half-monster. When you feel like a monster, you'll do anything to make yourself feel better. My abstinence from alcohol enabled me to feel superior to others. As on fire as I was for Jesus, I was turning into quite the Pharisee.

During my adolescence, Uncle Jerry was just at the beginning of a successful recovery from decades of alcoholism. Seeing his gradual transformation was really important for me. He opened up about how the disease had gotten him and what it took to overcome it. He let me ask as many questions as I wanted, and he answered me honestly. His transparency helped demystify alcoholism. Because he and my father had been occasional drinking buddies and he understood the challenges of alcoholism, he had a completely different perspective on the man than I did. "I was wrong about you, though," he said. "In the important ways you are nothing like him."

CRAFT BEER REVOLUTION

I can't find any data to back this up, but it seems that the craft beer movement in America predates most of the other examples of artisanal reawakening in our modern culture. I know it did for me. Craft brewers and home brewers innovate, creating new beer styles and paying homage to brewing traditions from throughout the ages. Beer is now more unique, healthy, and local than it has been at any time since the Prohibition era. After a century of cheap, watery, mass-manufactured, and homogenized beer, millions are connecting with this ancient brew in ways that reinforce community, responsibility, and even spirituality.

Historians believe the evolution of human societies from nomadic hunter-gatherer cultures to creators of villages, towns, and cities is directly related to the discovery of brewing and the realization that cereal grains could be cultivated. It's highly possible that brewing even predates baking. Agricultural advances may even have been motivated by the desire of ancient tribes to brew beer. Ancient beer and early versions of wine were certainly common by the time of the Hebrews' exodus from Egypt in 1446 BC. While Bible versions differ on how they render the Hebrew word, it seems that beer, or a drink very similar to beer, was commanded by God to be a part of the sacrifice offered in his tabernacle (Numbers 28:7) While moderation, responsibility, sobriety, and self-control are clearly extolled throughout Scripture, there is no scriptural or historical way to escape the fact that beer and wine have been a part of God's earth since the early centuries.

Prior to Prohibition, there were thousands of small breweries all over the United States. Beer was a highly localized product dependent on the cultural traditions of immigrants from around the world. Brewers developed styles based on the ingredients and technologies available to them. As the factory science of the Industrial Revolution began to impact brewing in the late nineteenth century, however, all of that began to change. Railroads transported goods over greater distances in shorter times. Prohibition, which began in 1920, created a perfect storm for the consolidation of brewing within only a few large corporations. Thousands of small regional breweries were unable to survive, and giants like Anheuser-Busch put many others that had endured out of business when Prohibition was repealed in 1933. While millions of American men were fighting in Europe and the South Pacific during World War II, the brewing giants lightened their beers to appeal to feminine tastes (and to save on ingredients). By 1978, there were only forty-two breweries in the U.S., and three of them—Anheuser-Busch, Miller, and Coors—were responsible for 99 percent of all beer sold. The United States had become known around the world as the source of the blandest, weakest, and most boring beer on the planet.

In 1978, the last vestiges of Prohibition were finally swept away when President Jimmy Carter signed a bill into law legalizing home brewing. Beer artisans, many of whom had been quietly experimenting with home brewing for decades, brought back brewing styles that had been dormant for seventy-five years. Several of these home brewers took their hobby to the next level and began the microbrewing revolution. Today there are nearly three thousand local and regional craft brewers in the U.S.

Among the millions of home brewers, craft brewers, and microbrew connoisseurs are countless numbers of Bible-believing, responsible, discerning Christians who see this return to quality, craftsmanship, and creativity as completely compatible with their call to community, hospitality, and joyful living. I've been enjoying this movement for twenty-two years as a brewer, a host, an appreciator, and a bit of a student. I'm happy to say I've turned twenty-one twice in this life, and I've still never been drunk and have no problem saying, "No, thanks."

CALFKILLERS

—◆—

I met the Sergio brothers at the East Nashville Beer Festival, an annual gathering of craft brewers and beer fans that takes place just a few miles from my home. When I saw their folksy, handmade booth with hand-carved filbert branches and lots of funky décor, I asked Dave Sergio about the "special" beer they were sampling and ended up having the kind of conversation you wouldn't expect to have at a beer festival.

"This one is called Cerveza De Jesus," Dave said, filling my small glass with a couple ounces of smooth, sweet, spicy ale. "We used all kinds of fruits and herbs that were around in Bible times."

"So it's named after *the* Jesus, not a baseball player or something?" I asked.

"Absolutely," he said, with a laugh.

"Are you a fan of Jesus?" I asked.

"Absolutely," Dave said. "My brother and I are big fans of Jesus. Some of the first beer we ever made was for a family wedding—just like him!"

Dave was laughing, but I sensed a sincerity in his words that his eclectic outfit (shorts over long johns, layers of different colored T-shirts, a puffy vest, and a ski cap) couldn't undermine. If Bob and Doug McKenzie (look up "Great White North," "Take Off," or *Strange Brew* if you're under forty) wanted to start a hipster indie rock band, they'd look to the Sergios for inspiration. I briefly explained I was writing a book about bread, coffee, chocolate, beer, and Jesus. "All things that make life worth living," Dave said. I asked if he and his brother would be open to doing an interview. He quickly agreed, and a few minutes later, he introduced me to his equally quirky and sincere brother Don.

Although their business is named Calfkiller Brewing Company, Don and Dave Sergio have never killed a calf. The name of their family-owned microbrewery comes from the Calfkiller River that runs through their hometown of Sparta, Tennessee, about two hours outside of Nashville. According to one legend, the name comes from the fact that before the city put in a series of small dams, the flow of the river was so intense in the spring that local farmers had to be careful so their small calves wouldn't be washed away. Another legend refers to a Native American chief who supposedly killed a settler's calf and started a war. The Sergios aren't sure if either story is true, so they thoughtfully included references to both in their logo.

Don and Dave share the easy rapport that only brothers can have—but few do. They finish each other's sentences and manage to be downright hilarious without ever cutting each other down. They are the youngest of six siblings, born in Wisconsin but relocated to Sparta as children. Like their older brothers before them, Don and Dave started working for their father's construction business when they were very young. "I think the last time I watched Saturday morning cartoons was when I was ten," Don says. "My dad expected us to work. He'd explain how to do something like lay a hardwood floor, and we'd just do it." They developed serious carpentry skills, which they turned into careers in construction, though Don spent some time on the road with a rock band in his early twenties.

Their "I can do that" attitude eventually extended beyond carpentry to brewing beer and roasting coffee. After offering me a cup of coffee made from beans Don had roasted just a few minutes before I arrived, he showed me a wood and metal contraption—two perforated metal plates attached to a broom handle—that was the first device he fabricated for roasting. The larger roasting vessel Calfkiller uses for its coffee is fabricated from sheet metal, scrap parts, and a gas grill.

The story of Calfkiller Brewing Company is similar to that of most other microbreweries in many ways. The brothers' brewing hobby escalated, enabled by their gift for inventing and innovating. I'm not sure how many brewers built the structure that houses their equipment with their own hands, using leftover materials from construction sites, but the Sergio brothers did. Their large family and tightly knit group of friends served as a more than adequate proving ground for their growing passion. Early batches were for family functions like weddings and parties. For several years, Don and Dave worked all day at construction sites and then all night at their makeshift brewery. In 2009, however, they decided to go pro. "Our plan was to make our full-time job [carpentry] into our part-time job, and our part-time job [brewing] into our full-time job." The process wasn't nearly as smooth as they expected.

The good folks of Sparta, perhaps with their Bible Belts cinched a notch or two too tight, refused to grant Calfkiller the commercial brewing license to which they were entitled. Despite clearly written laws that allowed for their plans and an official legal opinion from Tennessee's attorney general, the brothers were forced to sue the local beer board for their permit. "The judge sat there and looked at the paperwork,"

Don recalls, "and said 'Why are we here?'" It was pretty handy that Don had a pocketful of hops and barley when he took the stand. When the judge presiding over their case asked him, "What is beer, actually?" Don was ready. "It's just four things," he said, showing the judge the contents of his pocket, "barley, water, hops, and yeast." "All those things come from God," the judge said. "I don't see a problem." The beer board was told to sign the permit, and it hangs proudly in the Calfkiller brew house to this day.

During a two-hour tour of the brewery—which was hands-down the most entertaining such tour I've ever experienced—the brothers referred to the natural, God-given qualities of beer several times. As irreverent as Don and Dave may sometimes be, the faith their Catholic parents passed down is alive and well and informs everything they do.

The Sergio family helped establish the first Catholic church in their deeply Protestant part of the rural South. "It was a few families, a trailer, and a priest," Don recalls. Growing up in the Bible Belt, the Sergio boys were surrounded by evangelical kids who had a very different response to church. "The kids I went to school with seemed more—I don't know—fiery about their faith," Don says. "I was wondering what they were getting that I was not. I told my mom I wasn't getting anything out of church sometimes. She asked me, 'What are you expecting to get out of it? You're supposed to give.'" Don clearly paid attention to her words. The generosity of spirit that flows from him and his brother is palpable.

Don and Dave are excited about expanding their business to include coffee roasting, mainly because it allows them to support Nathanael Yoder, a local Mennonite missionary who lives and works in Costa Rica. "He went there to be a missionary," Dave explains, "and ended up buying a coffee plantation and providing jobs for the people he was serving." Calfkiller buys as many of their beans as Yoder's ministry can supply.

It is clear that Don and Dave Sergio approach their brewing business — which now produces up to a thousand gallons per week and is available in ninety-five locations around Nashville, Sparta, and other Middle Tennessee towns — with unabashed joy and enthusiasm. The brothers concur that there are always risks associated with being in the beer business. "All things in moderation, including moderation," is one of their mottoes "Most of the time, we need to live our lives without overdoing," Don says. "We can't eat a massive steak every night because that would kill us. But sometimes you just have to eat a massive steak — because you're alive and you can! It's the same with beer."

THE BLACK ABBEY

When I heard about a new craft brewery in Nashville named The Black Abbey, I was intrigued but suspicious. I assumed — correctly, I was to discover — that the name was a reference to Black Cloister, the monastery associated with Martin Luther and the dawn of the Protestant Reformation. Was there really going to be a Lutheran beer company in my hometown? If so, I thought, they had better make the best beer around.

A quick glance at the brewery's website confirmed the intentional association between the brand name and Luther, but the articles there pointed to a much deeper understanding of the significance of the cloister (later renamed Lutherhaus), which became famous for fostering community, conversation, fellowship, and learning during the formative early years of the Reformation. The Black Abbey Brewing Company is intent on crafting quality Belgian-style ales—which they believe are similar to the ales brewed by Luther's wife, Katherine von Bora—and on paying tribute to the life and words of Luther and John Calvin. So yes, Nashville now enjoys the presence of a truly reformed brewery as part of its thriving craft brewing community. And their beer is excellent.

The Black Abbey is located in an industrial park behind a shopping mall on Nashville's south side. It doesn't boast much vibe on the outside, but inside, visitors are greeted by a small chapel-like tasting room replete with long reclaimed wooden tables and a bar with a church-like arch behind it. Gothic hanging lights (purchased from an old Baptist church) and heavy oak beams complete the sitting area's décor, with an expansive brewing factory surrounding it. The tap handles are shaped like stained-glass windows, and the beer names and descriptions are loaded with references to the monastic life and European church history. On my first visit, I was there to meet Carl Meier, one of The Black Abbey's owners.

Carl started brewing in 1994 while attending Cornell University. Though he was raised in the Presbyterian Church, his faith had little to do with his interest in brewing at first. "In college I was the guy who tried to drink as much as I could as cheaply as possible," he says. "I grew up in the church, was always at church, and then I went off to college, and there were all these people from different racial, ethnic, and religious backgrounds. I wasn't a part of any religious community while in college. It wasn't until after I was married that I got back into church."

"It's true what they say," Carl continues. "All that wander are not lost. I might have been misdirected for a while, but I think it really affirmed in my own mind that the human condition is fundamentally broken, and that even if you're lost from the fold for a time, you're never really lost. I feel like I was that lost sheep Jesus talks about in Luke 15 that gets chased down and then returns to much rejoicing."

Carl married shortly after college and moved to Nashville. He and his wife visited several churches, trying to find something that fit both of them. After spending time in a home group with a couple from Covenant Presbyterian Church, the Meiers began attending the church and eventually became members. Carl was later asked to become a deacon, and while on the board, he met Mike Edgeworth, a fellow deacon, a home brewer, and his future business partner.

"Covenant had a big role in bringing me back to my faith," Carl says. "I think it's a fairly common experience. Kids go away to school and kick things around for a while. Then once they become grown-ups, they realize, *Hey, I need to stop acting like an idiot. I need to put my big boy pants on*. That's what brought me back. I think my times of wandering made my belief system stronger and more confident in the end."

Carl had been brewing for years, spending some time in a home brew club that included many of Nashville's best. Although he assumed he was the only brewer at his church, he discovered at a diaconal icebreaker meeting that several of the men were avid brewers. He and some of his new church friends started dreaming and scheming about opening a brewery. One Halloween night, it came to him all at once. "It was one o'clock in the morning, and I was cleaning up," he recalls. "I remembered that the next day was Reformation Sunday and wondered if I was supposed to wear red to church, or was that Pentecost Sunday? Then it occurred to me, *Martin Luther was a monk!* So at two thirty in the morning, I was up reading everything I could find about Luther and texting the other guys, *I got it!* I had brewed an Abbey ale, and that was it."

Already a fan of Luther's theological impact on the world, Carl began to uncover stories about the Reformer's connection to brewing—and beer's connection to the Reformation. Before meeting Luther, Katherine von Bora had been a Cistercian nun cloistered at Nimbschen Abbey. She and eleven of her fellow sisters, possibly influenced by the spreading rhetoric of the Reformation as it pressed against both political and theological abuses within the Roman Catholic Church, desired to leave the convent. Mother Superior refused. Though the penalty for leaving a convent, as well as for harboring runaway nuns, in those days was death, local food merchant Leonard Kopp helped the twelve sisters make their escape and brought them to Luther and his associates in Wittenberg for protection.

Several myths have evolved about this bit of Reformation intrigue. One, despite its complete lack of historicity, became Carl's favorite. "According to this legend," he says, "the nuns hid in barrels and were floated down the river." The sisters had been brewers, and so it seemed reasonable for the legend to claim that the barrels had been used for gruit beer—a brew in which a combination of botanical herbs and flowers is used for bittering instead of hops. Because hops had been outlawed by the church, gruit beer was common throughout the Holy Roman Empire and was directly related to the church's heavy taxation of brewing and its multifaceted control of society. "The legend has it," Carl says, "that Katherine was in the barrel Luther pulled out somewhere downstream." Carl began experimenting with gruit beer, and he named his first batch "Katherine's Escape," humorously connecting his brewing with his favorite Reformation legend.

Luther, then in his mid-forties, and Katherine, then just twenty-four, were married two years later, after great consideration and discussion. Though several of his friends and coconspirators opposed the union on the grounds that it might undermine the efforts of the Reformers, and Katherine took her own time deciding whether or not she would accept his proposal, Luther famously took his father's advice and married Katherine. On June 13, 1525, the outlawed ex-monk and the runaway nun were wed.

While the union of Martin Luther and Katherine von Bora may have begun as a pragmatic affair, it is clear from many of Luther's remaining letters that the two eventually developed a deep and abiding love. Luther publically esteemed his wife in ways that challenged the patriarchal tendencies of sixteenth-century Germany, extolling not only her cooking and brewing prowess but also her financial wisdom, intellect, hospitality, and humor. His "dear Katy" was an avid gardener, growing in her own garden nearly all of the food that was served on their table, and a warm host to the many boarders and guests who sheltered under the roof of Lutherhaus. Katherine, a licensed brewer, exercised the brewing rights on the property and produced what became known as the best beer in Wittenberg. "She sold beer out of that facility," Carl says with a laugh. "Luther never took money for his ministry or for his writings, so you could argue that Katherine financed the Protestant Reformation on the back of a brewery in the monastery where Luther became a monk. It's a ridiculous, unbelievable story, but it's awesome!"

Carl's respect for Martin Luther, John Calvin, and their contemporaries is authentic and deep. He pointed me to Jim West's fantastic book, *Drinking with Calvin and Luther!: A History of Alcohol in the Church*. The way the leaders of the Reformation took Jesus out of the shadows of politically corrupt and powermongering church leaders and made his words and work accessible to the common man is clearly inspiring to Carl and his partners. By associating his brewing with this aspect of church history, Carl seems to fuel his once dormant faith. He and his partners see a real connection between Luther's efforts to show hospitality, challenge traditional thinking, and bring people closer to God. Their cleverly worded manifesto is posted on their website: "Luther's commitment to transforming something distant and unattainable into a comfortable, meaningful part of daily life sparked a massive social, religious, and political reformation. Luther believed we should drink for joy! We at The Black Abbey Brewing Company second that wholeheartedly!"

THE SCIENCE AND THEOLOGY OF BREWING

Brewing is both artistic and scientific. For many brewers over the last several thousand years, it has also been spiritual. Brewers have long honored the mystery in the process, even as they search for new and unique ways to practice their craft. The ingredient list is surprisingly simple: water, barley (or wheat), yeast, and flowers. The process is critical.

The grain must first be malted by exposing it to just enough moisture so that the germ inside starts to grow. The hull cracks, and the starchy endosperm undergoes its critical transformation into sugars the plant would normally use for food. The process is then halted by kilning, or roasting, the malted grain. Varying the grains and roasting times creates a range of colors, from pale straw yellow to deep ruby black. Flavors range from mild and sweet to rich and bitter.

To make beer, the malted grain must be cooked in water that is no hotter than 170 degrees Fahrenheit for a specific amount of time. This process creates a sweet barley tea called wort, which must be brought to a strong rolling boil for the next critical step in the scientific process to occur: the sugars are transformed into a state in which they can be effectively fermented. During this stage, hops (the female flowers of the Humulus plant) are added to the sweet wort. The volatile oils in the hops do different things at different temperatures, and hops are thus added at different times during the boil. Hops added early provide bitterness; hops added later provide flavor; hops added after the boil stops provide aroma. Hops also act as a natural preservative.

The temperature of the wort must be reduced to about seventy degrees, and then the yeast is added. Yeast cells exist everywhere in nature and are constantly transported by the slightest breeze or contact with insects, animals, or people. Until relatively recently, brewers had no idea where yeast spores came from or exactly what they did. They did learn, however, how to partner with the mystery in the pursuit of different flavors and colors of beer. If I leave my sweet wort exposed to the air, yeast cells and other microbes will find it and ferment it. The results, however, could be terrible. By choosing my yeast carefully and taking great pains to keep everything clean and temperature controlled, I can control the fermentation process. When the conditions are perfect, the yeast cells consume the sugars in the wort, converting them into carbon dioxide and a relatively low amount of alcohol. The cells reproduce rapidly until they reach a certain saturation level in the beer, at which point they become dormant and settle to the bottom of the fermentation vessel.

The wort is now fully fermented beer, rich with the nutrients imparted by the grains and yeast and purified by the presence of alcohol. In the Dark and Middle Ages, beer was safer to drink than water. In his wonderful book *The Search for God and Guinness*, Stephen Mansfield unearths the fantastic history of beer in general and the story of Arthur Guinness and his heirs in particular. Guinness was a strong Christian whose beer was developed as a service to his fellow Irish brothers and sisters and as a healthful, wholesome act of worship.

In many parts of the world, beer has been a dietary staple for centuries. Historically, the low alcohol content of many varieties made it a preferred breakfast drink for children before school. Even the Puritans who landed at Plymouth Rock did so in part because they were running out of beer on the Mayflower! Beer was a dietary staple of the first American settlers.

Followers of Jesus have been brewing beer for centuries—usually following the same basic technique I follow when I brew at home. The tension between Christianity and alcohol is relatively recent—maybe as a result of the removal of beer from the context of its creator and its purpose.

A TOAST TO DISCERNMENT, DISCRETION, AND MODERATION

I realize alcohol is a touchy subject for many people, especially evangelical Christians. Almost everyone I know has been impacted by addiction in one way or other, and the biblical admonishment to avoid drunkenness and addiction is clear. Many of my close friends and people I admire greatly choose not to drink for health, family, or even devotional reasons, and others sometimes drink too much. I have Christian friends who are active alcoholics. It's heartbreaking to see these ever-present reminders of humanity's brokenness. Anyone who is not thoughtfully concerned about the risks associated with alcohol is either naive, deceived, or addicted. But should this concern cause complete avoidance? Every time I get in a car, there is a risk I might not leave it alive. Should that keep me from driving or riding in one?

A significant tool in my ongoing recovery from the pharisaical tendencies of my youth has been the example set by many great people of faith who have cultivated balance in their relationship with alcohol and have enjoyed it as unto the Lord. It's easy to categorically consume or deny something. It's far more challenging to know when to participate and when to abstain. For the last century, many Christians have decided alcohol is just too dangerous to leave to discretion — even as many of them slather more pork gravy on their biscuits or eat another slice of chocolate cake. We have stigmatized drinking but have allowed for the massive overconsumption of sugar, fat, and salt — all substances that are probably killing more people than alcohol. Discernment is a skill that must be cultivated and practiced within the context of community. Discernment enables me to grieve with those who mourn and to dance with those who celebrate. At times, a loving sensitivity to the struggles or woundedness of others demands that I say no to a certain food or drink. But discernment also allows me to enjoy a fuller experience of the blessings God provides.

When I was nineteen, I fell in with a new group of friends from Warehouse Church, an upstart inner-city church in Aurora, Illinois, that quickly became my spiritual home. Comprised mostly of musicians, artists, and misfits who wouldn't feel comfortable in a traditional church, the culture at Warehouse encouraged discernment, service, accountability, and transparency. Whenever I started acting like a Pharisee, my friends would call me on it. One of them, Randy Kerkman, taught me more about being a friend than anyone else had at that point in my life.

Randy was a bit older than me and way cooler. He was an excellent guitar player and had graciously lent his talents to help my little band sound much better than it deserved. He shared personal stories about overcoming temptation and healing from mistakes of the past. He talked to me like a brother. We laughed a lot. Once, he called me out when I wasn't acting like a true friend. I had never had a friend like Randy. The investment he made in me caused me to seek out other friends and to open up to being known by others for who I really was, not just by my carefully crafted image.

Randy lovingly challenged me on my legalism about alcohol. He said it was totally fine if I didn't want to drink, but I should think carefully about whether I was afraid to or thought it was a sin or thought I would automatically become an addict like my father. The key, he said, is to remain accountable to friends, to maintain self-control, and to know when it's better to skip it altogether. I agreed. I started to realize my legalism was based on fear.

Around the time of my twenty-first birthday, Randy bought me my first beer. I was house-sitting at 412 for my grandparents, so he and a few other friends from church came out for a little party. "If you're going to try a beer," he said, "I'm going to make sure you learn to like the good stuff." He'd brought a few varieties of Samuel Adams—one of the first craft brews available in the Chicago area. "Here," he said as he opened one and poured some in a glass. "This should be the cheapest beer you ever drink." He pointed out the different flavors and gave me a brief primer in craft beer. He poured a taste of Hacker-Pschorr Weisse and explained what wheat beer was all about. We finished with a stout I wanted to like more than I did. "You'll develop a taste for it," he said. "Just stay away from the cheap stuff."

It was sound advice.

Beer, chocolate, bread, sex—it can all be a source of great God-given joy, pleasure, and comfort, or of personal destruction. When the pleasure blessings of God are disconnected from their source and purpose, they can become sources of bondage, pain, and death. There is no good thing aside from Jesus that sin can't twist into a pair of handcuffs. But for me to avoid all blessings because of my need to practice discretion feels disrespectful of the giver, like never riding the bike my mother gave me because I might fall off.

I believe beer has been an important tool used by God in the process of conforming me to the image of Christ, as Romans 8:29 describes. Jesus made wine — good, strong wine — at a wedding (John 2) because he wanted to reveal something about himself. However, he also raised the bar for our treatment of others. According to Jesus, it would be better for a person to be thrown into the sea with a millstone tied around his neck than to cause another person to stumble (Luke 17:2). That "stumbling block" rationale was central to my abstinence position for many years. As I grew older, though, I was challenged by the fact that despite the risk, Jesus still made all that wine. Despite all of its warnings about addiction and drunkenness, the Bible paints a clear picture of drink as a blessing when used appropriately. Despite the millstone imagery, God still commanded Aaron and the priests to pour "fermented drink" on the altar along with the grain and the lamb and the precious olive oil (Numbers 28:7).

IN TROUBLE AT CHURCH

I was asked to join the elder team (which in our church meant I was one of the pastors) at Warehouse Church when I was just twenty-six years old. Many of us have heard of a nondenominational church, but Warehouse was led by a team of men from different theological and cultural backgrounds. We occasionally disagreed over theological concepts like eternal security, election versus free will, speaking in tongues, prophecy, eschatology, and the methodology of the administration of sacraments, but what we had in common was much more important.

Because our church was located in a part of Aurora heavily populated with alcoholics and homeless people and those who were in one stage or another of addiction recovery, we agreed to maintain a sensitivity to alcohol use. Our church's official position on the consumption of alcohol was centered on discernment, self-control, sensitivity, and caution. We could not teach that alcohol was inherently bad from a biblical perspective because we couldn't find Scripture to back that up. As pastors, though, we agreed not to have alcohol at any church events and to remain accountable to each other regarding our own drinking decisions.

At that time I rarely drank beer. In July 1997, however, I got in big trouble with a group from our church after someone put a six-pack of nonalcoholic beer in one of the coolers at my twenty-seventh birthday party—which took place at my house and wasn't a church event. I hadn't put the "near beer" in the cooler, but in hindsight I'm glad someone had.

A few people at the party—folks whose perspective was similar to the one I held a few years earlier—were profoundly offended. Gossip started to spread, and the truth was distorted and exaggerated. You'd have thought I was doing keg stands in the church parking lot for all the heat that came my way. In truth, I never even drank one of the "near beers." But my critics maintained that because it was my house and my party, and because I was a pastor, I should have made some kind of public statement that all beer drinking was evil—even nonalcoholic beers, I suppose. The controversy grew, and the elders (all of whom had been at the party) felt the need to call a churchwide meeting to discuss the issue openly. Randy Schoof, the founding pastor of the church, invited a couple of other local pastors to join us for accountability and advice.

The night of that meeting is one I will never forget. I was embarrassed, even ashamed, and felt like I should just cave, apologize, and swear to everyone there that I would never have a beer again. More frightening was the way I was tempted to step down from the elder team and retreat from a life of transparency and accountability altogether. I was still learning how to have deeper relationships, especially with other men. This kind of controversy made me want to go back to being one of those dudes who shows up at church but lives life on his own terms the rest of the week. I had tasted too much of what was possible, though. I couldn't turn back. I knew I needed this community, pain and all, more than they needed me. My brothers on the elder team made it clear they had my back, and this was going to be one of those messy things that happens when you're part of a true community.

The core members of the Beer Opposition Party (my name, not theirs)—many of whom were close friends I cared for

deeply and still love to this day—took the position that
our church should officially condemn alcohol and that the
pastors should take a public vow never to drink again. Tears
were shed. Apologies were made. But my brothers on the
elder team would not agree to make mandates where the
Bible does not. We were willing to increase our sensitivity
to the ever-present stumbling blocks that came with inner-
city, fringe-type ministry, but we would not "add to the
law," as Schoof put it. A few people left the church over
the conflict, which made me sick to my stomach. But in
the end, I learned several critical lessons I wouldn't trade
for anything. People are more important than my liberties,
and discernment is more important than the convenience
of adding to the law. Also, some people just leave churches
when things don't go their way.

Bill Cross was one of the guys from Warehouse Church
who was a perfect example of why such a ministry is so
important—and why it was important for a self-righteous
Pharisee like me to serve there. Bill struggled to fit into
mainstream culture. He described himself as a "run-of-
the-mill, drunken, dope-addled dumb-butt." But he didn't
use the word *butt*. It was easy to judge Bill as being a bit
of a basket case. When our church was first established, a
group of us met him at a local dive bar called Malo's during
a concert by a Christian heavy metal band called Sacred
Warrior. Some of the members of the band were members
of our brand-new little church, and all of them were friends.
I was too young to get into the bar, so the band snuck me
in the back door to work at their T-shirt table. The core

members of our new church were all at a terrible bar in a bad part of town, watching a group of our friends play heavy metal music. It seems like the kind of place where Jesus might have shown up.

I have a vague memory of meeting Bill that night, but it was a conversation he had with Randy Schoof that changed his life. After that night at the bar, Bill started showing up at church, and a few months later, he made a decision to give his life to God and to plug into our tribe for good. I believe Bill, like most people who go to bars, went to Malo's that night in search of community. I'm so glad he found a family in the process.

THE SACRAMENT OF SAVORING

Individual tastes are fascinating, exciting, and frustrating things. My exploration of artisanal things has heightened my awareness of the power of taste — for good or ill — in many different aspects of the human experience. Tastes can bring people together, or they can become splinters that keep people apart. Until we cultivate a taste for a thing, we will not seek it out, value it, or take it into ourselves. Once we cultivate a taste for "finer" things, however, we run the risk of becoming arrogant, self-important, and dismissive of people who haven't yet cultivated those same tastes. There are some tastes that matter — that are either inherently good or bad for the individual and the people surrounding him or her; other tastes don't matter at all. Sometimes it's difficult to know which is which, and the necessary discernment can be impossible to master outside of the context of community.

Some tastes are easy to acquire, while others require careful cultivation. Few children need much help to cultivate a taste for white bread, sweets, pop music, or cartoons. A love for whole grain bread, spinach, classical music, or good movies, however, requires an intentional cultivation of taste. It is one of the saddest ironies of the fall of humankind, I believe, that the things we love most easily are often the worst things for our mental, spiritual, and physical health. The things that improve our health, sharpen our minds, enrich our faith, and embolden our service are often initially repulsive. Cultivating a taste for the good, the true, and the beautiful is what mentors, pastors, teachers, gurus, and friends can encourage us to pursue, as we do the same for them.

I was in high school before I realized that my eclectic taste in music was a direct result of my lack of community with other kids my age throughout my childhood. I had little or no cultural frame of reference as my preferences developed. As a result, I enjoy music from a variety of cultures. My preference for honest, constructive lyrics was cultivated by exposure to people and ideas that mattered to me. My spiritual framework acts as a filter through which I observe life. Some of my artistic preferences—as both a creator and consumer of art—are purely based on aesthetics; others, however, are grounded in the morals and ethics of my faith. I have an extremely difficult time separating the art from the artist. It's hard to admire the work of a person I cannot respect.

A few years ago, my dad and I attended an event called The Science of Beer at a museum in Nashville. The organizers set up booths that demonstrated different scientific aspects of beer and brewing, but the real draw was the chance to taste different brews from around the world. Exhibitors at one booth handed out small strips of paper and asked us to put them in our mouth and describe the taste. My dad tasted nothing. I tasted a slight bitterness. Slight differences in our DNA actually changed how, or if, we perceived the same chemicals.

That little experiment reminded me of an experience in ninth grade Biology 101. After we used small applicators to put different unmarked liquids in our mouths, we reported on what the tastes were and where we noticed them on our tongues. I was working with my lab partner when we got to the last flavor. I put the swab in my mouth and tasted nothing; my partner put it in her mouth and started gagging. "It's bitter!" she said. I tried again. Nothing. I reported the strange phenomenon to my teacher—a grump by the name of Mr. Mott. He put a swab of the stuff in his own mouth, recoiled from the bitterness, and then chided me for being a smart-aleck. He asked me to try again, handing me a little cup of the substance. I poured the liquid into my mouth. I gargled. Nothing. Mr. Mott seemed to think I was kidding around, and it made him mad.

The next day, he began the class session by saying, "I owe Mr. Thompson an apology. I did some research last night and found that a small minority of people can't taste quinine" (the chemical used to identify which part of the tongue recognizes bitter flavors). "So it seems," he continued, "that Mr. Thompson was not acting up; he simply can't taste correctly." I was surprised to learn of my disability. "He probably doesn't taste anything exactly the same way other people do," Mr. Mott said. I believe he was wrong about that. Most food doesn't contain quinine, and I seem to taste bitterness fine in other foods. But I suppose I have a higher tolerance for it than some people.

The tongue gathers chemical information from food or drink, and the nose harvests olfactory signals, but there would be no taste without the brain. An infinitesimal hybrid of chemical signals and corresponding translations are what determines a person's functional tastes. The texture of a food or drink—the way it feels as it moves around in the mouth—affects how a person understands that food's flavor. The pain associated with hot peppers is integrated by the brain into the process of determining the flavor of spicy food. For primitive man, a sweet taste signified a food rich in calories. A salty taste might signal the presence of critical minerals or other nutrients. Bitterness warned of poison. Subtle differences in flavor and smell help a person distinguish between the sourness of rotten food and the sourness of a lime. Over the last century, scientists have even identified specialized taste receptor cells for fats and for savory meats and vegetables.

When we eat or drink, these different receptors are stimulated, and our brain interprets the signals, triggering a feeling of either satisfaction or warning. When we eat sugar, salt, or fat, our digestive track sends powerful feel-good signals to the prefrontal lobe of our brain. This stimulation of what psychologists call the brain's pleasure center creates feelings of euphoria, comfort, and well-being in the exact cerebral area that reinforces behaviors, establishes habits, moderates self-control, handles emotional responses, and forms memories. Our brain recognizes this pleasure and remembers what caused it. Our brain then craves that pleasure again and again—and does so in a chemical and psychological way that is considerably more powerful than conscious thought. As those foods are eaten and the pleasure signals flow through our blood, they actually function in much the same way as drugs, alcohol, sex, and gambling. They don't call it comfort food for nothing. Millions of people regularly self-medicate their anxiety, fear, or depression with sugar, salt, or fat instead of heroin, cocaine, or liquor. We don't need any help developing a taste for the things that hurt us.

Processed foods tend to have flavors that are far more intense than natural foods and emulate nutrition that is not present. Our brains don't know any better, and they continue to crave foods that have little or no nutritional value and are high in empty calories based on taste alone. How can the sweetness of fresh snow peas compare to the sweetness of a piece of candy? It can't. Like an addict who is developing a high tolerance for a certain drug and increasingly needs larger doses to feel the desired effect, our sensitivity to sweet, sour, savory, salty, fatty, and spicy foods decreases over time, meaning we need more and more of those foods to feel satisfied.

If we work at it, we can train ourselves to appreciate flavors that repulsed us at first. I hated asparagus as a kid, but now

I genuinely love it. The same is true of sushi, spinach, beer, and coffee. I remember once taking an accidental swig of coffee, thinking it was hot chocolate. I thought I was going to die. In time, though, because I chose to, and because I surrounded myself with people who exposed me to the highest quality coffee, I developed a taste for it.

There are obvious nutritional benefits to learning to like healthier foods, but this process of cultivating taste has powerful ramifications that extend well beyond food or drink. Living in community, opening myself up to the scrutiny and discomfort of accountability—these are things that do not come naturally to me. I have developed a taste for them, though.

CULTIVATING GOOD TASTE

I asked George Howell how he cultivated such a fine coffee palate. "By doing it," he said simply. "The more you do something in a disciplined manner, the more you are able to do it." George benefited from the influence of Erna Knutsen, who George says is the first specialty coffee importer in the United States and someone the entire specialty coffee world owes an incredible debt to for her work in the field. Erna had taken George to Kenya and introduced him to people who showed him the Kenyan way to cup coffee. "It was different," he said of the particular technique the Kenyans used to analyze the fine flavor notes of their coffee, "and it taught me a more thorough discipline to pick out great coffees."

While George was familiar with standard Kenyan AA coffee, at that point in his career he had only tasted bulk beans— massive blends of beans from various farms throughout the country. While cupping one particular Kenyan estate's beans, though, he was overwhelmed by the taste of fresh blackberries. He started eating real blackberries just to confirm what it was he thought he tasted. "I almost OD'd on blackberries," he says, laughing. "I just couldn't believe it. A Kenya AA from a single co-op, when it's done perfectly, can blow you away."

Developing a sophisticated palate—whether in the service of coffee, wine, beer, chocolate, or spiritual formation— requires extensive practice and derives benefits from mentorship. Randy Kerkman introduced me to the subtle flavors of bread in a German Hefeweisen and an oatmeal porter. "Bread is just beer gone wrong," he said. "Taste it like a good rye bread—notice the flavors." Thanks to his coaching, eventually I could. Scott Witherow, with his extensive culinary training, not only can discern the subtle flavor notes of chocolate; he knows how to work with them. Conching the chocolate longer (kneading the cacao paste) or roasting a certain type of bean at a specific temperature, can accentuate desirable flavors and reduce undesirable ones. Like music or fine art, the cultivation of good physical taste requires mentorship, motivation, practice, and patience. The road to cheap, processed food—high in fat, sugar, and salt—is wide, as are many of the people who travel it, but the road to good taste and discernment is narrow, and fewer people choose to travel it.

Discernment must also involve the ability to say no. Even the best wine can be ruined if we drink too much of it. I remember one of my youth leaders talking about our spiritual diet. We discussed the impact of everything we allow into our hearts and minds—the Bible, films, music, conversations with friends, our daydreams, what we learned at school. Someone made the observation that you don't usually see athletes or models gorging on junk food because their physical fitness is critical to their identities. That comment stuck with me. Thirty-some odd years later, I still frequently have to pause and ask myself if the food I am eating, the drink I am consuming, the movie I am watching, or the conversation I am participating in is consistent with the person I want to be. Are my actions backing up the things I say I believe? Discernment demands I not only learn to taste the difference between the good, the true, the beautiful and the foul, the false, and the ugly, but that I exercise the personal discipline to say no to the latter.

I have a friend in the music business—I'll call him Wayne—who knows more about wine than just about anyone I know. Wayne's career is centered on a particularly conservative segment of the Christian world, so he has to be careful not to offend anyone with his passion for wine. He's not just a wine guy, though. He is preparing to be a certified Level 1 sommelier. Wayne has traveled the world studying wine. He has invested thousands of hours in the cultivation of his ability to taste and to communicate about what he tastes. He leads a growing wine club in Nashville and has even been invited to instruct the staff of J. Alexander's on tasting, serving, and pairing fine wines.

I had dinner with Wayne and some other friends in California last year, and much of the discussion centered around wine. I asked Wayne how he had developed his sophisticated palate. "Gradually," he said. "You don't start off with a bold, complex wine like a Cabernet. You start with a more delicate wine with simpler flavors. You learn to recognize the flavors and the smells, and to describe them. You might notice berries or toast. Then you just keep doing it."

I asked Wayne if wine had ever felt spiritual to him. "All the time," he said. "Something I learned when I was with some winemakers really paralleled my spiritual walk beautifully. When grapes are picked, they're not washed. They are put into the destemmer and crushed. Whatever is on them—the dirt, the smoke, the rock, whatever it is—that's what makes them what they are. During fermentation the alcohol gets rid of anything that's harmful, and that is a great spiritual parallel as well. No one said, 'That grape is dirty; it needs washing.' They are simply plucked and put in. That's so beautiful."

If you put an unlabeled glass of wine in front of Wayne, he will be able to tell you the type of grape, the country it comes from, the age, and maybe even the vintner. Level 3 sommeliers, which Wayne doubts he will ever become, can identify any wine from anywhere in the world, down to the specific region or even vineyard, and the exact year it was bottled. There may be no better example of discernment in the food world than a Level 3 sommelier.

Wayne's training is both for personal satisfaction and for the purpose of training others. "Wine is food" he says. "Wine is meant to accompany a meal. It's always meant to be served with food. That's the old-world way. None of the great winemakers set out to make the best wine in the world and get rich. They make wine to go with dinner." Wayne can help people choose the right wine to go with a particular food, as well as help people like me find a good wine for under twenty dollars.

I've grown up in a culture that gorges when it should learn to savor. I remember sitting in a McDonald's with my buddy Rob Anstee. I suggested we say grace before we ate our Big Macs. "I don't know," Rob said. "I think God might say 'Hey, I gave you perfectly good food, and you did *that* to it. Don't ask me to bless that mess. This is on you!' " So instead of saying grace, we prayed for forgiveness.

Cultivating good taste is a skill that tends to bleed from one area of life into other areas. As I spend time intentionally tasting new foods and talking with friends and experts about the flavors I might otherwise miss, my appreciation and desire for the good stuff only grow. Over the years I have noticed that as my discernment improves with regard to beer, coffee, and food, I also tend to become more aware of cheap teaching, weak ideas, poorly executed community, and shallow values. Then, on my better days, I actually find the strength to say no to those things.

But there's no silver bullet to subdue our taste for junk food, cheap beer, or plastic fellowship. If you want to have better taste, hang out with people who have better taste. If you realize you need to be spiritually and emotionally nourished by fellow pilgrims, then find those pilgrims and spend time with them.

Lots of time.

King David wrote, "Taste and see that the LORD is good" (Psalm 34:8). Jesus offered food and drink that would satisfy eternally to the woman at the well (John 4). He made good wine for a wedding party at Cana, when most of the partiers were too drunk to recognize its quality (John 2). Can you imagine how good any wine that Jesus made must have been? The inability of the guests to taste the difference in no way diminishes the goodness of the gift. The host of the party could tell, though he didn't know where the wine had come from. He credited the generosity to the groom. The servants knew the truth, though. They were the ones who filled the stone jars, and they were the ones who drew the wine from the jars and gave it to the host. Jesus' first public miracle—the first sign employed to reveal his glory—was to turn plain water into rich wine for an audience that could not appreciate it. Wow!

This passage challenges me every time I read it. Am I like one of the party guests, so drunk that I can't tell the difference between cheap, watered-down wine and the good stuff? Or am I a servant participating in the work of Jesus as he reveals his glory? John tells us that when the disciples saw what had happened, they believed in Jesus. I hope I would too.

COCOA BOURBON MILK STOUT

In 2007, after several years of reading and researching and feeling released from the strictures about alcohol I had placed on myself, I started stirring my own brew. I love the whole process. Even the science of it is worship for me. Each step of the process involves creative choices and hard science. The results can be fantastic or terrible.

When I brew, I enjoy the fact that I am engaging in a process designed by God, utilizing ingredients only God can make and scientific principles that point me to a pattern of grand design. When I serve homemade beer to friends and see the look on their faces as the fresh, wholesome flavor hits their palates, I feel like a kid bringing home a straight-A report card to his parents for approval.

Of the twenty or so beers I have made, my specialty has become my milk stout. Though it is dark in color, it is mild and rich in flavor and has a smooth mouth feel established by the addition of lactose during the brew. Lactose, which is milk sugar, is not fermentable. It adds a smooth richness. Lately I've been experimenting with some other ingredients. Scott Witherow had given me a pound of Olive & Sinclair cacao nibs he had aged in a bourbon barrel, and I added those nibs to the wort for the last fifteen minutes of the boil, then put in a half pound of my own freshly roasted coffee for the last five minutes of the boil. The result, a beer I call my Cocoa Bourbon Coffee Stout, is good, if you savor it.

Really good.

I like to think that God has a picture of it hanging on his refrigerator.

Sometimes the flavors we savor are right there on our tongues, while other times they are wrapped up in the stories and relationships around the table and are savored in our hearts. We recently celebrated our oldest son's twenty-first birthday with no small amount of fear, trembling, and joy. I promised our kids that if they refrain from drinking until they're twenty-one, I will buy them their first drink and do my best to ruin them for the cheap stuff. So as we sat at an upscale pub in East Nashville and looked at a menu of boutique cocktails, nice wines, and local beers, I remembered my own slightly belated twenty-first birthday party at my grandparents' house at 412. Grandpa Holton came out to the back deck with a bottle that had a faded handwritten label on it. "Happy twenty-first birthday to my first grandson!" he said. "I bottled this wine when you were a baby. I think it's time we open it." I remembered the bottle well. Grandpa opened it and poured a small bit into the cups of all of the adults, including mine and my new bride Michelle's. I'm not sure what rhubarb wine is supposed to taste like, but the flavor in my mouth was something like a cross between turpentine, lemon juice, and soap. "Some wines don't get better with age, I guess," my grandpa laughed.

I think that may have been the best drink I've ever had.

Chapter 7

TIME BEGAN IN A GARDEN

We have a long box, roughly the size of a pig trough, in our backyard. For about six years, it was my gardening space. I planted tomatoes, peppers, and sage in it. Some years, it did really well; other years, not so much. Last year, however, my family petitioned me to give them one square foot of space for a couple of strawberry plants. We got a few little berries from those plants last year. This year, however, without prodding or planning on our part, the strawberry plants have taken over the whole box! Not only that, but they are producing some of the juiciest, sweetest berries I've ever tasted. I don't get many because they are aggressively harvested and consumed by our youngest son, but I've had a couple. This morning, I grabbed one before I got in my car to head to work. It was perfect.

In the summertime, when I was a kid, the first thing Grandpa Holton did when he got home from work was head out to his garden. In his suburban Chicago backyard, he cultivated green beans, rhubarb, tomatoes, snow peas, lettuce, bell peppers, radishes, onions, broccoli, eggplant, cantaloupe, zucchini, cucumbers, various squashes, and more. My brothers and I were often asked to weed the garden, water the plants, and pick the ripe vegetables. I wish I could say I loved every minute of it. The truth is that I saw garden work as an unbearable chore.

One summer, I begged Grandpa to let me grow watermelon. He said he didn't think it would work well because of the climate, but I insisted. He gave me a small patch behind the pool. I planted watermelon seeds in a paper cup full of rich potting soil. I kept the cup inside, watered the seeds several times a day, and talked to them. I remember being so excited when the first little whitish-green shoot popped up. A few weeks later, it was ready to be transplanted into the hard soil of the garden. The plant grew quickly and impressively, and I tended to it every day. I kept its little square of earth free of every weed, maneuvered the vine to get the best sun exposure, and watered it constantly. Finally, after months, a single melon began to form. I went nuts.

Only one melon grew on that vine, and it stayed white all summer. It also grew in a perfect sphere instead of becoming the oblong shape I was expecting. "I'm not sure that's going to taste too good, Johnny," my grandpa warned. He could see how excited I was and didn't want me to be disappointed. By the time my birthday came in July, the melon was roughly the size of a softball. A month later, it was almost the size of a bowling ball and still bone white. I nurtured it throughout August. After rainstorms I went out and washed off any soil that had splashed on it. I loved that melon. On Labor Day, we had a big family cookout. I decided it was time to pick my watermelon and share it with the family. Grandpa cut it open with his big knife, and the flesh inside was bone white. It had no flavor at all. I ate the whole thing, savoring every morsel and imagining it was sweet and juicy. I was delusional.

I shared this memory with Grandpa recently, and he laughed. He's in his eighties now, and his dementia is getting pretty bad. He'll forget what I've just said but can remember things from the distant past. I asked him if he had grown up gardening. "Oh yes," he said. "My father always had a garden in the backyard. In fact, at one point we had an entire lot next to our house that was a big garden."

"Did you enjoy gardening when you were a kid?" I asked.

"Not that I can recall," he admitted. "I'm sure I would have rather been out getting in trouble. But later on, when I was on my own, I started gardening right away."

Grandpa didn't grow up on a farm. He lived in a suburb of Detroit called Ferndale, near 8 Mile Road. Long before the days of Eminem and gangs, 8 Mile was a quiet road, and Ferndale was a peaceful middle-class bedroom community. Grandpa's father was a salesman for an agency that placed ads in buses and trolleys. Sometimes Grandpa went to work with his dad, which meant jumping on bus after bus and changing out posters. Sometimes it involved getting off at certain stops and going fishing. Backyard gardening was not common in Detroit. "No one I knew had a garden but us," Grandpa says.

My brothers and I lived with my grandparents on and off for many years. In the summertime, our cousins and neighborhood friends came over to swim in the pool. My mother was in school, so it often became Grandma's task to prepare dinner. More often than not, she fixed whatever had come out of the garden that day. I remember a massive, deep skillet she would line with layers of sliced tomatoes, squash, eggplant, and whatever else she had. She topped it with tomato sauce and Parmesan cheese, making it into a sort of vegetable lasagna. Sometimes ground beef or chicken got mixed in. We had that a lot in the summer. We didn't always like it. I'd love a bowl right now, though.

Grandpa didn't believe the opinion of children should ever be a factor in what was on the table for dinner—unless it was that child's birthday. He would gladly make us sit at the table until long past dark if we failed to finish our food. I remember being stubborn about summer squash once. My brothers and cousins all finished their dinners and went out to the pool. I sat there, listening to them splashing around and having fun while I made myself gag on my dinner.

"You can sit there for the rest of your life," I remember Grandpa saying with humor, "or you can just learn to like it. You can learn to like anything if you put your mind to it." He was right. I love summer squash now.

At that point in my life, I was very connected to the food I ate. But by the time I was a senior in high school, a large part of my diet consisted of Snickers and Mountain Dew. I was as much a fast-food junkie as anyone I knew. I remember thinking a McDonald's McDLT was healthy because it had lettuce and tomato on it.

Like just about everything else in this world, our food system is broken. Our insatiable hunger for comfort, convenience, and security, combined with a complete separation from the natural and supernatural sources of our sustenance, leaves us fat and malnourished. A majority of Americans are overweight, and a third of Americans are obese. Food-related health problems, including heart disease, liver disease, diabetes, and various cancers, are closing in on smoking-related diseases as America's number one killer. My own relationship with food has frequently been far out of balance, disconnected, and unhealthy.

A FOOD REVOLUTION

It took watching a few documentaries for me to really begin to engage with the critical food conversations happening on the fringes of our culture. The frightening issues related to modern industrial farming practices, government food policies, genetically modified crops, and the critical degradation of the environment first registered with me when I saw films like *Food Inc.*, *King Corn*, and *Ingredients*. One documentary that really gripped me was *Eating Alabama: A Story about Why Food Matters*. In it, a young couple, Andrew and Rashmi Grace, move to rural Alabama and vow that for one year they will eat only food grown or raised within a hundred miles of their home. The things they and their audience learn about how difficult it is to do that, and how simple it could and should be, blew my mind. These films and books like *The Omnivore's Dilemma* by Michael Pollan and *Fast Food Nation* by Eric Schlosser are essential resources for understanding the issues. A chorus of voices is speaking out in ways that are finally reaching the mainstream of the culture. I feel like that guy in the choir who is mouthing the words as I learn to sing along.

I met Bill Guerrant at the Wild Goose Festival in 2013. He and I were speaking together on a panel about food justice. We ended up spending most of the day together, riffing on each other's ideas. Bill recently walked away from a thriving legal career in Tampa, Florida, to work the land of a farm that had been in his family for generations. In the midst of his transition from the courtroom to the garden, he also decided to enter seminary. "I didn't feel a calling to the pulpit or to be a pastor," he said, "but I did feel that seminary would help me understand what I was doing from a theological perspective." His thesis explores the writings of John Wesley and surmises where he would land in the contemporary food movement.

Bill and his wife, Chérie, are two of the best ambassadors for this movement I've ever met. Their motivation for organic, non-GMO farming holistically includes health benefits, spiritual benefits, ethical and environmental considerations, sound theology, and an appreciation for the enjoyment of good-tasting food. "We're trying to find ways to farm that heal the land," he says. "We are trying to restore and encourage local economies. We're trying to reintroduce people to what food is supposed to taste like and to concepts like seasonal eating." The Guerrants rotate dozens of crops, including broccoli, cauliflower, cabbage, peas, asparagus, sweet potatoes, squash, shiitake mushrooms, watermelon, and cantaloupe, and raise free-range chickens, pigs, and goats. "We don't use any chemical fertilizers or pesticides," he explains, "and we sell our food locally through farmers markets and onsite." The couple also hosts monthly conversations with members of the local community who are interested in transitioning to a healthier, more sustainable food life. "Some cities have a well-developed food community," he adds, "but we're in rural Virginia, and we have a pretty long way to go."

For Bill, food is a spiritual issue as much as a practical issue. "Being involved with creation and seeing creation as an ongoing process absolutely connects you to the Creator," he says. "What we're trying to do is what most believers and seekers are trying to do, which is to align our life with God's will and his purposes for this new creation." Bill is regularly faced with the obvious spiritual disconnect happening between people of faith and their food. "We're deep in the Bible Belt here," he says. "I bet that 99 percent of the people I come in contact with are Christians on some level. When you bring up issues about food, farming, or the environment, though, many of them withdraw from you. There's a general mistrust of environmentalism with many of these folks, and they are good-hearted people."

Bill believes this is partially the result of dysfunctional theology folks have inherited, including the idea that since God is going to cleanse the whole earth with fire soon, there's no reason to worry about the environment. Others take a more political approach, assuming anyone who raises environmental issues must be a godless liberal. For Bill, though, it all comes down to how one understands God. "One of the things that has changed me is coming to a better understanding of theology," he says. "The idea that we should be encouraged by wars and disasters or by increased crime and environmental degradation because it means Jesus is going to return—that just makes my skin crawl. These are good people, but this is a very bad, harmful, deceived way of understanding creation. And it is not at all what the Bible teaches."

Bill is also aware of a major disconnect between Christians who are not concerned about their food and those in the alternative food movement who are not concerned about God. He says someone once remarked that plenty of people honor creation but don't honor the Creator, and plenty of people honor the Creator but not the creation, but we needed to model the importance of honoring both.

"I'm convinced that as Christians we should be at the forefront of every effort to improve the world," Bill says. "To treat our bodies as the temples God made them to be. To join with God in the ongoing redemption and restoration of creation that I believe began at the resurrection and will ultimately be manifested in the union of God and earth as described in Revelation 21." Bill is no naive hippy. He is a thoughtful, good-natured, articulate advocate. I found myself wanting to write down everything he said.

"It's not enough to say we want to eat better because we want better-tasting food and want to be healthier," he says. "We should say we want to eat better because we want better-tasting food and want to be healthier *and* want to be part of making the world a better place because that's what the Creator expects of us. We want to be a part of something that good and that beautiful."

GANGSTER GARDENING AND ORGANIC URBAN RENEWAL

In 1988, the band Talking Heads released a wonderfully odd little pop song called "[Nothing But] Flowers" that imagined the devolution of the then-thriving American urban sprawl back into a botanical garden of Eden covered in flowers. The song was a hit during an era of unbridled corporate expansion and massive commercial development. The roaring '90s were just around the corner, and the last thing anyone but David Byrne could imagine would be a reverse gear on progress.

Over the last few years, as reports mount of massive urban decay, deepening poverty, and global recession, it seems some parts of the song are coming true.

American cities are plagued with abandoned factories and desolate neighborhoods. Detroit, once a beacon of American commercial power, has become an international symbol of postapocalyptic, capitalistic blight. The concrete crumbled, and the steel rusted. The weeds have taken over. Yet revitalization projects have been going on for a while, and progress is being made.

According to a wildly popular 2013 TED talk by self-styled "guerilla gardener" Ron Finley, 26.5 million Americans live in "food deserts." This means residents are unlikely to have access to healthy, fresh, wholesome food. Many poor urban neighborhoods have been colonized by fast-food joints and convenience stores, and several generations have grown up without a taste for vegetables or the slightest idea how to prepare them. These densely populated wastelands have significantly higher-than-average rates of obesity, diabetes, and other food-related and preventable diseases. Finley and his group decided to take this on by turning public land — like the patches of dirt and grass between the sidewalk and the curb — into food-producing gardens or "food forests."

Urban gardening is becoming more popular every year. Apartment dwellers and young homeowners are exploring concepts like vertical gardening and square foot gardening in order to raise their own food. Nashville recently passed an ordinance to allow homeowners to keep chickens in their yards as a source of eggs. Homegrown food is flavorful, inexpensive, and fun. But while young, educated urban hipsters discover the joy of gardening as a hobby, for low-income inner-city families, the ability to grow and cook fresh fruits and vegetables can be a matter of life or premature death.

One Nashville group called Hands On Nashville has launched an urban farming program dedicated to teaching children how to grow and appreciate vegetables. Through actual gardening and classroom teaching, Hands On Nashville is cultivating a taste for real food in children who might otherwise continue the cycle of fast food and poor health they were born into.

Finley adds a certain gangster swagger to his fresh-food evangelism, equating the growing of vegetables and fruit to printing your own money and sticking it to the system. He uses terms like *ecolutionary* and *gangster gardening* to relate to urban youths who are given few opportunities for productivity. Nonprofit ventures like Greening of Detroit are inspiring and empowering thousands of urban poor to plant trees and gardens in the neglected acres that typify the modern-day Motor City.

Bill Guerrant credits Wake Forest Divinity School dean Gail O'Day with saying that for many young people, food can act as a "gateway drug to social justice." Growing food is one of the most therapeutic and empowering things many people ever do. It's good for the body, the mind, and even the soul. If dreamers and revolutionaries are looking at the problems in places like South Central Los Angeles, urban Nashville, and inner-city Detroit and finding answers in seeds, dirt, hard work, and community, maybe that's where followers of Jesus should be too.

WE AFFORD WHAT WE VALUE

Food is essential to survival, and yet it is one of the first areas where I tend to cut corners. Healthy food costs more than factory food and can be harder to find. Healthy food takes much more work and costs more to produce than factory food. I have made many excuses to justify my unwillingness to invest in healthier food. I'm prone to the influence of marketing. I wonder if it's really that much better for us. I think of all the other things I have to pay for. It occurred to me a few years ago, however, that whether we're talking about a corporation, a nation, or my family, our budget reflects our values. We can say we care about the things of God all day long, but our checkbooks often paint a different picture.

When I mentioned the unfortunate cost of healthy food, Bill gently and graciously opened my eyes with some research he had uncovered while working on his thesis. The data showed how little we Americans pay for food as a percentage of our monthly expenditures. "The percentage of its income that our society spends on food is the lowest of any society in history," he says. According to Ronald Stone's 2001 book *John Wesley's Life and Ethics*, in Wesley's day, people spent nearly everything they earned on food. "Today in the U.S," Bill says contrast, "a mere 10 percent of Americans' disposable income is spent on food, down from nearly 30 percent in 1950 and 17 percent a mere thirty years ago—and for food eaten at home the cost percentage is only 5.7 percent. By comparison, Europeans spend about 25 percent of their income on food."

Also, the actual price of the food we see in the grocery store or on the menu does not represent its true cost. We must take into account hidden liabilities, including environmental degradation, fuel costs, poor conditions for workers and animals, harmful pesticides, and poor nutrition. "Much of the cost has been prepaid by our taxes," Bill says, "which are funneled to the industrial producers in the form of subsidies." These subsidies make industrially grown food appear cheaper than it really is and gives massive corporations a competitive advantage over farmers. Other costs are deferred. Food-related disease and obesity are growing at alarming rates as we gorge on cheap food.

Many of us have lost our taste for wholesome food, having reprogrammed our brains to crave incredible amounts of sugar, fat, and salt. When I was a kid, I got to choose what the whole family had for dinner on my birthday. I remember that on my eleventh birthday, I chose a Kraft macaroni and cheese dinner. I could have asked for anything, and that was what I came up with! Grandma looked at me quizzically. "Are you sure?" she asked. I assured her I was. I partially wanted it to be easy for her, but I also really liked macaroni and cheese. About 20 percent of the backyard was a garden full of fresh tomatoes, cucumbers, zucchini, peppers, snow peas, broccoli, and eggplant, but I chose a cardboard box with the word *cheese* in quotation marks. Who knows what that golden goop actually was.

How many times have I done that since? I wonder. *How often have I turned my nose up at truly good food because something else was cheaper, more convenient, or covered in powdered cheese sauce?*

We have four kids. Buying healthy, organic, non-GMO, free-range food is expensive. We have expenses like medical bills, insurance, a high-speed Internet connection, and other nonnegotiables. We can't afford to eat like the Guerrants eat. Or so it appears on the surface. Bill has found some impressive evidence that eating healthier, more local food may not cost as much as we've been led to believe. "For the vast majority of people in our society," he says, "an increase in the amount spent on food simply won't crowd out the other necessities of life. In fact, the additional cost of eating a healthy diet has been estimated to be, on average, $1.49 per day."

Just $1.49 per day? That's less than our Internet connection. A few months ago, Michelle invested in the services of a nutritionist. Her theory is that cultivating a taste for more wholesome food is likely to reduce medical bills over time. We're not brand-new at this either. It's not like we're transitioning from eating White Castle every night to strict veganism. Over our two-plus decades together, we've been gradually waking up to the value of healthy eating and then finding a way to afford it.

BACK TO THE GARDEN

The farm we lived on when I was a kid was a nightmare. It felt haunted. We were isolated and felt that way. The land was owned by a doctor, who had plans to build fancy houses there. My buddy Tim's dad actually farmed the fields and shared the earnings with the doctor. Our job was basically to take care of our tiny house and a few outbuildings. None of the quaint, pastoral images one would associate with farm life bore any resemblance to the reality of life on that piece of land. We had some chickens and a useless old steer. There was an orchard of apple trees and a hedge of raspberry bushes, but what I remember most was hard ground, high weeds, and clouds of dust whenever the tractors ran. My mom cultivated a small garden with the experience her father had passed on to her.

There was something about it, though. The land in West Central Illinois is rich. There was a dump on that land—a place where someone had created a pile of old appliances, furniture, and plastic. We found snakes there, and even wild dogs once in a while. The dump was like a gaping, festering wound carved in ground that wanted to be beautiful. Over time, I noticed weeds, shrubs, and saplings start to grow thickly around the edges and then up through the middle of the dump. Vines spread their tendrils across an old washing machine. Slowly, relentlessly, the earth seemed to be healing itself. Those weeds were like white blood cells rushing to fight off an infection.

My mom managed to make things grow in the hard ground, mostly out of necessity. She harvested tomatoes, potatoes, onions, green beans, and berries. At the end of the summer, she got out the pressure cooker and a bunch of glass jars and canned up a lot of the produce so we could eat it through the winter. She was about twenty-eight years old, with four little boys who also managed to grow in the dirt of that farm.

We went back for a visit several years later, and the dump was almost completely covered. In 1999, my band was booked to play in nearby Peoria, and we scheduled a trip to visit the scene that served as the inspiration for our most recent record, simply titled *Farm*. The little house was still there but had been overrun by wild animals. The outbuildings were gone — even the big barn. No trace of it remained. The dump was gone too. The land was healing, and so was I. The memories of that place and the abuse that had occurred there no longer lived in the front of my mind. In fact, that whole dark period of my childhood was feeling more and more like a bad movie I had seen at some point in the past.

My mom has a little plaque that reads, "Time began in a garden." What a profound truth! God designed things to grow, to survive, and to thrive. The ground is designed to nurture things, and seeds are made to grow, whether they are stray dandelion seeds or watermelon seeds. Some seeds don't do well in certain soils or climates. Some come back year after year, while others must be replanted each spring. Fruit-bearing plants require a healthy water supply, while crabgrass can thrive in near-desert conditions. Most desirable plants require regular care and attention, while thistles can find one-sixteenth of an inch of dirt under some cracked pavement and spring up into majestic, four-foot-tall terrors.

Many of Jesus' stories use agricultural imagery to help his audiences make connections to their spiritual lives. He talked about reaping and sowing, harvests and mustard seeds, good soil versus rocky soil, and predatory birds. Each of us is planting, nurturing, and harvesting day after day. There is no sideline. There is no retirement. I want to be engaged in that story. I want to be actively involved in the crafting of the garden of my heart and mind, not passively watching it become overrun with weeds or genetically modified techno-plants. This kind of hands-on farming is exhausting work, but it is oh so rewarding. There is nothing quite as satisfying as serving someone a meal you cultivated with your own hands. Not only does that kind of food taste better—naturally and spiritually—it is thrilling beyond words. I have truly never felt more alive than when the fruit of my life was blessing someone else. It's addictive. Like Grandpa hitting the garden when he got home from work, I want to make sure I'm tending the garden of my soul every day. Both kinds of agriculture are rewarding, even when they are difficult.

My son gave me another strawberry from our little trough tonight when I got home from work. It was perfect. I have dreams of establishing a garden in our Nashville yard. I hope to get some chickens. I love making salsa from tomatoes I planted, nurtured, and harvested with my own hands. On a purely material level, our homegrown food tastes better and is healthier for my family and for me. As critical as increased awareness and engagement with our food supply is, however, there is much more to it. When we lose touch with our food sources, we lose touch with the ground, the seed, the water, and the work. The same is true of our spiritual lives. I believe God wants us to be actively involved cultivators, not just passive, ignorant consumers. As painful as the process may be, he blesses me abundantly when I allow him to prune the weeds in my heart.

Chapter 8

ARTISANAL MUSIC AND THE TUNE OF COMMUNITY

In 1997, I found myself sitting in the office of a counselor trying to comprehend the disaster happening to my dream business and the psychological devastation it was wreaking in my heart and mind. "You know, John," Russ the therapist said as I looked back at him blankly, "the downside to getting to do what you love for a living is that if it goes south, you have nowhere to turn for release." Music had been everything to me since I was a kid. I made it my career and my identity. It was the center of my social, professional, and spiritual worlds. Now that my music business was going up in flames, I was too. I had nothing to do for fun, nothing to relieve the worst stress I had felt since I was ten years old and hiding from my father on that farm. I knew a lot about music by the time the tragedy that sent me to Russ came on me, but there was something very important between the grooves that I had yet to understand.

I first learned to be a coffee, chocolate, bread, and beer snob by becoming a music snob.

I'm sorry — "music appreciator."

Music has never been an optional accessory in my life. From the moment I got my first pair of bulky radio headphones, I learned how to drown out the noise of the world by simply turning up the volume. We moved so frequently when I was little that I never had a chance to form lasting friendships, which meant I had no real guidance about the music I should or should not like. I developed an extremely diverse musical palate.

My mom got me an Isley Brothers T-shirt at a resale shop when I was seven, so when I heard them on Soul Train, they instantly became my favorite band. I saw Johnny Cash's show on TV with lots of static when I was even younger. When I heard him sing "A Boy Named Sue," he became my favorite. I heard Kansas sing "Dust in the Wind" on the radio, and they became my favorite. The Doors seemed to understand darkness. The Who seemed to get my anger. The Beatles were magical. My mom had some "Jesus music" records by artists like Jamie Owens, Love Song, and Honeytree, and I found songs to love on those records too. Mom's music sounded like it came from an alternate reality—a world that was peaceful and serene. I couldn't relate to that world, but it sure sounded nice. When I was ten, my world was haunted by fear, tension, insecurity, and God. I discovered a late-night gospel radio show out of Chicago that aired on a station my radio picked up only after dark. There was something beautifully desperate about that music. The pastors were also singers, and they sounded like they might explode from the joy they felt in the midst of trials and pain.

James Brown, Tom Petty, Aretha Franklin, Barry Manilow, Queen, Rev. Milton Brunson, the Bee Gees, Bob Dylan, the Mighty Clouds of Joy, Merle Haggard, The Beach Boys, The Clash—they all crackled through those awkward headphones, chewing through nine-volt batteries, blocking out the craziness happening around me, and giving me a feeling of virtual community. Music was the language of my tribe, and I was listening under the door, pretending to be in the room.

I didn't know about the supposed divide between sacred and secular music until much later. To me, all music was essentially spiritual. The only questions were which spirit was behind it and what was it accomplishing. There was the spirit that drove my mother, my grandparents, and the people at our little church to be kind and loving and sacrificial and generous, and there was the spirit that drove my biological father and so many other people in the world to behave in selfish, violent, unjust ways. There was a kind of love out there that inspired people to lay down their lives for others, and there was the kind of love that people sang about on the radio that seemed to be about using another human being's body and soul to satisfy your own lusts. There was light, and there was darkness. The light seemed to be where I might someday find peace, purpose, and meaning. But the darkness was always hanging around in the background, offering to scratch the itch it had revealed. In my mind, music was true or false, good or bad. I had ears to hear songs that spoke to my soul.

Much of the music I obsessed over echoed with the pain and fear I felt in my gut every day. While some songs pointed to the way things should be, most focused on the way things actually were. The sexual urges of a young man are real, but meditating on songs that reinforced the myth that sexual satisfaction was the highest priority in life did nothing to move me out of my darkness. I started to suspect that the musical diet I was consuming contained both nutritious elements and poison, and it was time to learn the difference. By the time I was twelve years old, I found myself seeking out deeper truths. I craved music that wrestled with the big questions about human nature, hope, justice, and the way things were supposed to be in my own heart, not just the external world.

When we lived on the farm, we went to a small rural school. Every so often, the teacher brought in a book catalog, and we could choose something from it. I once ordered a book about Stevie Wonder, and he immediately became my favorite. Something about knowing the story behind the artist and the meaning of the songs lit me up. The deejays on the radio never talked about what a song meant. I called a college radio station once, and they put me on the air. "That song you just played, 'Blinded by the Light,'" I said. "What does 'Wrapped up like a deuce, another runner in the night' mean?" The deejay, who had seemed like a cool girl as I listened to her, was caught off guard, and her answer was abrupt. "I have no idea," she said. "I just listen to the music."

What a cop-out, I thought. No one just listens to the music of a song and ignores the words. That's not even possible. It's like saying you can take the chicken flavor out of the chicken soup.

When I discovered artists I suspected were onto something deep and true, I wanted to know everything about them. I wanted to know the musical influences that inspired them. I wanted to know what they believed about God and death and love and purpose. Sometimes I was inspired by what I learned; often, I was let down. I have never been good at appreciating the art of an artist I can't respect. It feels like eating an apple that grew from a tree planted in a sewer.

That little Stevie Wonder book opened me up to the realm behind the music—the artists themselves. Stevie sang about "Superstition" and "Living for the City." I read about the mean streets of Detroit, the struggles faced by black Americans—struggles I had never seen in person—and I understood his music better. That book led me to *Rolling Stone* and other magazines. I wanted to know more about the artists. Were they telling me the truth? What were these songs about? They had to mean something.

I once saw a movie on TV about Johnny Cash. He talked about overcoming addiction and making mistakes, and about how Jesus helped him. I remember fantasizing that Johnny showed up at our house. In my dream he was a head taller than my six-foot-four father. Johnny took the old man outside, beat the crap out of him, and took me away to raise me right.

One night on the way to Cub Scouts, right before we all ran away from my father, my mom asked, "If you had to go on a long trip, with no time to pack, and you could only take what would fit in one bag, what would you want to make sure was in that bag?"

"My headphones!" I said without even needing to think about it.

A few days later, I was baptized at a church picnic. I had been baptized Catholic as a baby, but I was making a conscious decision to accept Jesus and to make a public statement about it. My brother Jeff and I went through a few classes at our little country church, then got baptized with some other folks in a pond. My grandparents came from Chicago for the event. They gave my brother and me orange duffle bags with our initials engraved on them as baptism gifts. I remember thinking they were strange gifts until a few weeks later when everything I owned was being lugged around in mine.

Grandma also gave us a Realistic tape recorder and a few cassettes. Mom had been getting a little concerned about some of the music I was listening to. I seem to recall her hearing me sing "Psycho Killer" by Talking Heads and asking me what the heck I was listening to. I had found a college radio station out of Peoria that played some really weird music. I liked it. She just heard her nine-year-old, with massive headphones bungee-corded to his head, singing "Psycho Killer, bla bla SAY, fu fu fu fu fu fu fu fu fu fu better run run run run run run run away!" I guess I can see why she was concerned. So Grandma went into a Christian bookstore and said something like, "My grandson is listening to some troubling music." I imagine her pulling out a piece of paper with the intel she had gotten from my mom. "He likes the music of Talking Heads, The Clash, The Doors, Billy Joel, and the Eagles. Do you have any Christian music that sounds like that?" The store clerk recommended an album called *Straight On* by a band called DeGarmo and Key, and a few other tapes as well. Grandma bought them for me, and a couple of others for Jeff. She made the mistake, though, of telling us they were Christian rock tapes. When you're developing a taste for "Psycho Killer" and your grandma gives you Christian rock tapes, well, let's just say we weren't supereager to check them out.

Within a couple of weeks, we were on the run. I had my orange duffle bag, my headphones, my tape recorder, two tapes, some comic books, a notebook, a pencil, three or four Star Wars action figures, a spaceship toy, a Pink Panther coloring book, my sleeping bag, some new pajamas, my Stevie Wonder book, a Bible, and my pillow. Our first stop was the battered women's side of the Wayside Cross Rescue Mission in Aurora, Illinois. Mom said we couldn't tell anyone what our names were, and she couldn't tell us what city we were in. Jeff and I had slept for much of the trip and had no idea how long it had been since we left the farm. It was dark when we got there, though, and most of the people we saw were black. "I know where we are," I told my little brother as I thought of the pictures in my Stevie Wonder book. "We're in Detroit."

The time we spent at Wayside Cross was odd. We spent our days either hanging around the resale shop where my mom was working or playing pool with men who were in the addiction recovery program. We heard some wild stories from those men. I remember being in the resale shop one day and finding an old acoustic guitar to play with. My mom had a classical guitar I had played a few times, but I really had no idea what I was doing. An older nearly blind black man was sitting by the door. He heard me messing with the guitar and offered to show me how it worked. He tuned it and showed me how to play an E chord and an A chord. "That's all you need to know to play the blues, kid," he said. I asked him about the blues, and he told me some stories. The only thing I really remember, though, is him saying the blues were about people telling stories that didn't have happy endings. "Why would anyone want to hear those stories?" I asked. "To know you're not the only one feeling the weight of the world," he said. *The weight of the world,* I thought. *Wow, what a concept!* That knot in the pit of my stomach, the fear I felt at night, the suspicion that Mom would change her mind and take us back to my father—maybe that was "the weight of the world." I never knew for sure if the tear that fell from that man's unseeing eye was because he knew from his experience something of what I was going through or because he had allergies. He said a short prayer for me, asking God to protect me from all harm. Then he told me to start singing my story.

I immediately became a fan of the blues.

One day, probably out of boredom, I finally put the tape by DeGarmo and Key in the tape recorder and hit Play. It stopped me in my tracks. The music was a blend of progressive rock and blues. The singer's voice was soulful and guttural, and the guitar work was incredible. Most importantly, though, the record was dark. It started with a song about the day that the city of Jericho fell. It then careened into a frenetic "art rock meets blues" song called

"Living on the Edge of Dying" that, even though I was only ten years old, I felt could be my theme song. "Go Tell Them" was about evangelism. "Bad Livin'" was a testimony song that sounded like it could have been written for my father. "Long-Distance Runner" was about not giving up. "Let Him Help You Today" sounded like the band was singing to me alone. The entire album pulled me in. Listening either on the tinny speaker of the tape player or in a single earphone in mono, the poor fidelity didn't matter. I was listening under the door again. It wasn't just that the lyrics were Christian, though they clearly were. The lyrics were true. They were good. They were giving me hope. I sang along. I wrote out all of the lyrics by hand in my notebook. I studied the layers of instruments, trying to identify each one. *Straight On* was like my own musical Rosetta Stone. It was like God was saying, "I haven't forgotten about you, Johnny. Hang on. It'll get better."

A month or so later, we were living at a Christian campground called Riverwoods, nestled along the banks of the Fox River north of Aurora. Riverwoods was a camp for low-income, at-risk youth whose parents couldn't afford traditional summer camp. Every Sunday evening, a busload of kids from the housing projects and poor neighborhoods of Aurora, Elgin, and other Fox River towns showed up. Though my brothers and I were not technically a part of the camping program, the counselors let us participate in the activities and mealtimes while my mom worked on administrative stuff in the office. Almost all of the kids were African American or Hispanic, and we had a blast with them. It was hard to make friends for a few days and then see them leave, but knowing another busload would come in each week made it kind of exciting. We were still in hiding. No one in our family could know where we were, and we weren't allowed to give people our full names. The nights were scary. I was afraid my father would find us in the woods at that campground, and his .38 would finally be used. Daytime at the campground, though, was pretty fun.

One afternoon when the campers were gone and the counselors were resting, I was in the screened-in porch of our cabin listening to *Straight On* and drawing. One of the counselors walked by, heard the music, and stopped. "You like DeGarmo and Key?" he asked. I was shocked. I had no idea anyone else had heard of them. "If you dig that, I have some other records you should hear." I followed him to his cabin, where he had a little record player and a dozen LPs. For the rest of the day, I felt like I'd fallen down a rabbit hole. Bands like Resurrection Band, Servant, Jerusalem, Daniel Amos, and Petra, along with solo artists like Phil Keaggy, Larry Norman, Randy Stonehill, and Mark Heard, all became part of a new sound track in my heart. I was speechless. Chris, the counselor I knew as Gizmo, was letting down a musical ladder into my pit and helping me crawl out. He let me listen to those records as often as I wanted, but at the end of the summer, he left the campground. It would be a couple more years before I found those records again. They were not sold in record stores and not even available in most Christian bookstores. They were too rock and roll for most Christians, and the rock-and-roll world ignored them altogether. "How can this be?" I said, enraged. "Someone has to do something about this."

HOUSE CONCERTS: KINDA LIKE CHURCH

Over the last decade, as the floor has fallen out of the music business, many musical artists have found it more and more difficult to fill traditional venues, and record labels have had to focus their resources on the more popular artists. Countless musicians—many of whom had the backing of record companies in the past—have found themselves unsigned, independent, and desperate for work. The era of the house concert was born.

I've seen artists who at one time would have been playing in theaters or at universities sitting in someone's living room with an acoustic guitar and a dozen fans. On the surface, this may seem like a major fall from grace, but the truth is that many artists are discovering a great deal of creative satisfaction, artistic freedom, and even financial value in this counterintuitive format. House concerts may not be bigger, but for many artists, they are definitely better.

My wife and I have performed on big stages in front of thousands of people, as well as in living rooms. In truth, the first time I performed in a house concert setting was every bit as unnerving—maybe even more so—than any big stage I had ever played. The big concert environment provides several effective barriers between the performer and the audience. There's the stage, the rows of monitors, and even the manipulative lighting. The stage allows artists to present a much cooler version of themselves than you're likely to see elsewhere. You can't see the food stuck in their teeth or the oil on their faces. The artist is far more vulnerable in a house concert, but so is the audience.

Kinda like church.

When I'm performing a house concert, I can tell which songs really connect with people and which ones are just OK. I've seen people doze off, and I've seen people tear up. For the most part, people are there because they want to be, and they're often much more engaged in the performance than spectators at a club or in a stadium. Sometimes you can even hear people sing along. You rarely see people checking email.

Fans are also as generous with their finances as they are with their attention. It's not uncommon for a new fan to buy every bit of music we have with us. Fans who are becoming friends because of the intimacy of these experiences can be extremely generous with their tips. If a person feels well served, honored, and blessed by the performing artist, he or she tends to see a healthy donation not as a cost of entry but as an expression of support and solidarity.

Kinda like church.

When I was thirteen, I saw one of my favorite bands, The 77s, perform on the big stage at the Cornerstone

Festival. I was electrified. In 2007, I saw Michael Roe of The 77s perform in my East Nashville living room. It was a thrill of a different kind, but no less exciting. House concerts get to the nub of the artist-fan relationship in a way that has been all but obliterated by the modern concert industry. Thousands of musicians are returning to the troubadour model of yesteryear and finding it's pretty cool. They may not be getting rich or famous, but many are experiencing something much more satisfying than money or fame: They are finding purpose, community, fellowship, and challenge in a small space with a handful of people and no obstacles to intimacy.

You know what I'm going to say . . .

Kinda like church.

NO SUCH THING AS SECULAR

I believe music is so powerful because it is essentially spiritual. There is more going on than just a reflection of sound waves into human ears. Music hits the heart first and then the brain. It impacts us emotionally far more than rationally. It can move us physically, causing us to dance or to relax or to throw our hands in the air. Music reconnects our normally disconnected emotions, intellects, and bodies. It's like food for the spirit. Sometimes it's good food; sometimes it's not.

Music is also inherently communal. Although I was listening alone on my Realistic headphone radio, the beat I heard connected me to thousands of other people. Music creates moments in which we feel less alone. It can draw tribes together, providing each member with a common rhythm. It can be used to motivate us to either seek the good of others or trample others in a mad stage rush. As it connects each of us to our own bodies, minds, and spirits, it also connects us to the bodies, minds, and spirits of others. This is scary for many people, with good reason, but I'm convinced God designed it that way on purpose. An intimate love song can connect a man and his wife in a deeply passionate way, and it can provoke sexual attraction between strangers on a dance floor. It can turn a roomful of people into a cohesive, spiritually engaged, worshiping organism, or into a self-gratifying and objectifying orgy. To discard music because of its potential for abuse, however, might be the greatest offense of all. It exists for a reason: We need it.

I started writing songs when I was about twelve years old as I learned how to play the guitar. I sang in the choir at church and at school. I struggled to be a good friend—having precious little practice as a kid—but I loved standing in a choir and singing along with a group. When I sang, I felt I belonged. When I was about fourteen, I started a "band" with my friend Rob and his drum machine. We would get together in his basement after church and pound out some terrible noise. Rob was always a much better musician than me. He tolerated my exuberance and got caught up in it for a while. Being in a band was really where I first learned to be a friend. As mysterious as music was to me, it made far more sense than other human beings did. Hanging out with four or five other people for hours at a time and allowing them to see past the carefully cultivated image I was projecting to the outside world taught me a lot about my own social shortcomings and my need for growth. No one knocks you off your high horse like a bandmate.

Over the next few years, I set about the work of figuring out who I was going to be. Music remained a constant presence. I discovered more interesting underground Christian music, lots of "normal" Christian music, and lots of interesting secular music too. I spent Saturdays riding my bike to the library, listening to records, reading about music, and writing stories, poems, and song lyrics. I went to the youth group at St. Mark's Episcopal Church, where a series of volunteer youth leaders took extra time with me. My musical obsession was encouraged and enabled. Every birthday and Christmas meant more records. I eventually found all of the records Gizmo had played for me in the cabin at Riverwoods, but I also heard truth coming through Tom Petty, the Eagles, Kansas, and The Police. To me, everything that was true was Christian. I didn't see a dividing line. But the artists who toiled in obscurity, doing what they did with no hope for fame and no respect from the world — they really became my heroes. It seemed most of them were doing their best to take Jesus seriously. I wanted to be like them.

One of those bands, Resurrection Band (or Rez Band, as many people called them), really rose to the top for me. Their music was hard, and their message was intense.

They tackled poverty, apathy, drugs, divorce, corruption, compromise, and temptation. They sang about war veterans coming home from Vietnam and comfortable Christians ignoring the pain outside their doors. They sang about South Africa's system of apartheid long before I heard anyone else sing about it. They sang about people with disabilities, depression, addiction, and rage. Every song expressed a gut-level confidence that Jesus knew about all of these broken people, cared desperately for them, and expected those who went by his name to love them on his behalf.

I found more music by DeGarmo and Key as well. I heard on the local Christian radio station that they would be doing an autograph event at a mall near my house. I couldn't get anyone to take me, so I walked the few miles, only to find when I arrived a long line I wasn't willing to stand in. Instead, I surveyed the area and guessed which door they would be coming through. I waited at that door for just a few minutes when a van pulled up and a group of cool-looking, long-haired guys with sunglasses got out. "Are you guys DeGarmo and Key?" I asked breathlessly. "Yeah," one of them said. "Walk with us." I almost fainted. I was talking so fast about how cool their songs were and telling them about Gizmo and Grandma and everything else that I almost forgot to breathe. As we walked, each of the four band members signed my *Straight On* cassette cover. We made it to their table where I had to leave. I added my own autograph above theirs, like I was in the band too. I still have that signed tape cover in my office. When I showed it to my boss on my first day of work at EMI Christian Music Group (now Capitol

CMG Publishing), Eddie DeGarmo just shook his head and smiled. It had been twenty-five years since he had signed that tape case. "That's wild," he said. "Wild."

Fortunately for me, Chicagoland had a Christian radio station that played this kind of rock, metal, and alternative music each evening from nine to midnight and every Saturday night. It took a little digging, but I discovered more artists who self-identified as Christians and others who sang more subtly about their faith and its impact on their worldview. Bands like The Call, After the Fire, and U2 were signed to mainstream labels and took a different approach than Resurrection Band's, but they were still singing the truth. U2, in fact, became my heroes in another way.

A girl from my church heard about U2 because she deejayed at her school's radio station. She noticed the biblical references, the social justice themes, and the unique, ambient musical style and figured I'd be a fan. She loaned me the band's *October* album, and I was floored. Here was a "real world" band singing worship songs, protest songs, hymns. and love songs—all from an obviously Christian perspective— in a way unbelievers didn't seem to mind. I was transfixed. When their *War* album was released, which included an interpretation of Psalm 40 as the last song, I cried.

Few of the kids at school had heard of U2. They were listening to metal and pop rock bands singing about getting laid and partying. But I was a fan. In fact, we had our first-ever computer class when I was in eighth grade. Our project was to tell an Apple II computer where to print X's and where to leave blank spaces so as to create some kind of design. My design, by far the most elaborate of any in my class, was "U2" with a line under it and then the word *War*—an approximation of the logo on their LP. I had to come in after class to finish it because of the detail. My teacher loved it, though. I got an A, and my design hung in the trophy case outside of the principal's office. A bully named Chris, who had an ill-fitting retainer, saw me looking at my accomplishment and said, with spit flying, "You like stupid music," then shoved me into the trophy case. I felt I had just taken one for the team.

I wrote band logos over everything I owned and made mix tapes for all of my friends. If there was a kid going through a hard time, I'd make him a tape. If there was a girl I liked, I'd make her a tape. I could use these songs to share my faith or speak out against something when I was too shy or afraid to talk. I probably made a hundred mix tapes between seventh and tenth grade. The last one I made was a one-hundred-minute collection of love songs for Michelle. There was some weird stuff on that tape—like The Waterboys and They Might Be Giants next to Mark Heard and Rez Band. I think I was trying to warn her about what she was getting herself into.

ALL I NEED IS SOME TRUTH

My stepfather taught me how to play guitar and let me listen to his records. Dad is an excellent guitarist and was a big fan of Phil Keaggy. Once we listened to most of Keaggy's instrumental *The Master and the Musician* record, and Dad pointed out different motifs and styles. The record, he said, was the sound track of his and my mom's courtship. That kind of freaked me out, but the music triumphed over my awkwardness.

Sometimes I'd bring Dad a song, and he'd show me how to play it. He had been in a band in the '60s that did covers and originals. He seemed to know everything. Once, I spent an entire rainy Saturday trying to learn the guitar solo in "Hotel California." I wanted his help, but he was gone that day. When he got home, I was at the end of my rope. I begged for his help. He came into my room, and I dropped the needle on the song. When the solo part came on, I played along until the point when two notes rung out at the same time. I could get about the first five notes but couldn't figure out how a human hand could play the rest. "Now, John," Dad said gently, without a hint of mockery or sarcasm, "you do realize they have two lead guitarists, right?"

In the fall of my freshman year of high school, I went to see Rez Band and The 77s at College of DuPage. The 77s modeled yet another way to artfully incorporate their faith into music. While Rez Band was highly confrontational about issues and integrity, making bold calls to action and weaving a long, powerful testimonial sermon into the middle of their rock show, and U2 cryptically referenced biblical images and thoughts in a way Christ followers would pick up but others might miss, The 77s were completely different. Lead singer Michael Roe took all of the tension associated with living as "a stranger in a strange land," internalized it, personalized it, and then let it explode out of him with poetic and dramatic flair. His lyrics were less obvious than those of Rez Band's Glenn Kaiser and less obtuse or political than Bono's. I determined that all three approaches were valid. The openness I had learned as a kid without a peer group now extended to this world of faith-fueled art. "Just give me some truth," John Lennon said. "All I need is some truth." I was cultivating a taste for art that reflected the fullest possible expression of truth and all of truth's ramifications.

The following summer, after hearing even more amazing music at the first Cornerstone Festival—including a surprise set by Kerry Livgren of Kansas that just about gave me a heart attack—I decided God wanted me to be an advocate for this music and these artists, on behalf of all the other kids who needed something more than the junk on the radio, something more than just an escape. Maybe some folks needed help developing a taste for this faith-based music, and I could be the one to help them do that. The music on the radio and on MTV went down easy, like macaroni and cheese or a Big Mac. But there was so much more out there.

Something even more profound than the discovery of new bands happened at that first Cornerstone Festival. As excited as I was about music, it had almost always been a solitary experience. It was me and my headphones, or me and my record player in my room, or me listening to Chicagoland's WCRM in my bedroom alone at night. The connectedness I felt was virtual. What I needed was real community. I wrote to bands when I could find their addresses, and there were few thrills as visceral as when one wrote back. It was like someone else tugging on the end of a rope that was tied to my heart.

I called and talked to deejays as they spun records—sometimes for hours. I subscribed to every music-related magazine I could find. These were my people, but they were not in my room with me—not in the way I really needed. I didn't realize it at the time, but music and the off-the-radar world that created and consumed it were pulling me toward the community experience I desperately needed.

I brought my girlfriend, Tina, with me to that first day of Cornerstone. She was a good sport about it, but once I hit that fairground and saw thousands of other people who were just as passionate about this Christian music as I was, I was gone. As The 77s played on the main stage, I kept pressing closer to the front and completely forgot about poor Tina. When Kerry Livgren of Kansas took the stage and connected the dots between his "Dust in the Wind" days and finding a real connection to Jesus, I exulted. This was my home planet. These were my people. I was actually there with them in the flesh. I never wanted it to end.

In a way, I got my wish. My first job was at a Christian bookstore, where I became the music buyer at age sixteen. Two years later, just after graduating from high school, I opened True Tunes, a music store in Wheaton, Illinois, that strived to be a Cornerstone-like connecting point year-round. Eventually, it gave birth to an international magazine, a concert venue, an independent record label, and a mail-order company. Someone once told me that in True Tunes, I had built my own little town and made myself mayor. I also kept working with my band, The Wayside. We got to open for many of my favorite artists when they came to Chicago, and we played local shows as often as we could. This faith-music life defined me. Pulling people together virtually and physically became my purpose in life. Music was the draw, but not the ultimate goal. We were confused and excited pilgrims, and life was so much better when we were together and a band was playing.

Music was also a powerful tool for the formation of my faith. I memorized passages of Scripture because artists had set them to music. I was challenged to confront poverty and injustice in whatever way I could by artists who introduced me to Compassion International and Amnesty International. When a songwriter spoke in an interview about a book that had been particularly influential in his or her life, I read it. Authors like Frederick Buechner, Brennan Manning, Francis Schaeffer, Henri Nouwen, Brother Lawrence, Thomas Merton, Philip Yancey, and countless others spoke into my mind and heart as records played in the background.

I used to say music had saved my life. That sounds romantic, like the kind of thing a rock star would say. The truth is that God saved my life, and he used deeply flawed, broken, hurting people to do it. Music was, and still is, a wonderful tool in his toolbox.

Fortunately for me, music wasn't everything.

When I was twenty-six, the world I had constructed for myself crashed and burned. My mentor and financial backer and I agreed to sell True Tunes to a company that talked of franchising and growth and expansion. I would be a minority owner of the new version of the company, and together we would take this alternative faith-based music thing to the mainstream. But within months, the new owners were shutting down all tangible aspects of the business—the print magazine, the concert venue, the record store—and moving everything online. I was devastated to have so badly miscalculated that deal. I couldn't listen to music or play music without feeling sick to my stomach. I had a splitting headache for months. I wasn't sleeping. Michelle could tell I needed help and loved me enough to push me to get it. I talked to my mom and dad, and they reminded me of a counselor I had seen a few times when I was a kid. They connected me with Russ, and I began meeting with him a couple of times a week. Russ was trying to help me find some kind of escape valve before I had a nervous breakdown.

"What else do you love besides music?" Russ asked. I had no immediate response. Just blank stares. "OK," he continued, "let's go back a bit." Russ knew all about my family's history. He knew about the hiding, the drama, and my mom's remarriage. He had helped my mom and my new dad as they built their hybrid family. This was a huge blessing because I didn't talk about my father easily or voluntarily. "Think back to before you kids and your mother went into hiding," Russ prompted. "What did you enjoy back then?"

"Star Wars," I said.

"That makes sense," he said. "Good versus evil, the salvation of the evil father by the brave son. I can see why that would have meant a lot to you."

Crap, I thought. I had never considered that my love of Star Wars was connected to my father. I told Russ about the day my father took my brother and me out of school to see the first Star Wars movie in a theater. My mom hadn't wanted us to see it because it was rated PG, but sometimes my father's sociopath needle swung over to "good dad mode," and he would make some grand gesture, like lying to teachers to get us out of school to see a movie our mother didn't want us to see.

Of course, we loved it. As soon as we got home, we found sticks to turn into lightsabers and started beating the tar out of each other. And the music! There were no VCRs or cable TV yet, so the only way to relive the movie was to play the sound track over and over. I have to dig for good memories of my biological father, but this was a defining one.

"I remember," I told Russ, "that he took us to see *The Empire Strikes Back* right before we ran away. At the end of the movie, when Darth Vader says those famous words to Luke Skywalker, 'I am your father,' I just about had a panic attack. For years, until the release of *Return of the Jedi*, I held out hope it was a lie. Darth Vader was the devil. He was just saying that to get Luke to give up. I told myself that for years, but deep down, I knew Darth Vader was my father too."

Russ said a lot of people collected Star Wars paraphernalia. He had seen a booth at an antique store and seemed to know someone who was an avid collector. "Maybe on your lunch breaks, you should go hunting for Star Wars stuff."

Obviously, Russ didn't know how obsessive I could be. Within weeks, I was collecting anything Star Wars I could find. I'd get a rare Boba Fett figure at Toys "R" Us for five dollars and trade it in at a comic book store for fifty dollars' worth of stuff. Before long, I had amassed an amazing collection. I imagine everyone but me knew this was a coping technique.

Russ also helped me reconnect with a love of cooking that had gone somewhat dormant during my pursuit of a life in music. "Cooking is great for creative people," he said. "You get to experiment and create and offer it to an audience." He was right. It's also far more productive than collecting toys. I started making my own tortillas and salsa, got further into craft coffee, and even did some gardening. It was around this time that I found myself in my kitchen talking with my friend John the baker about the history of bread. It seems there was yet another layer to this story that was only going to unfold if I allowed the True Tunes episode—the prequel, if you will—to roll the credits. A new chapter was beginning in my life, and while music would certainly be a part of it, it was no longer disproportionately central. I was starting to realize that my obsession with music, as well as bread and coffee, is really about my need to be connected to people.

Music, even instrumental music, is about voices. My son recently saw Sigur Rós perform ambient music to a stadium-sized crowd in a language he didn't comprehend. He described it as "worshipful" because of the emotions it inspired in his spirit. Often, though, music puts literal voices in our ear. It brings us ideas and cultures and accents and flavors that might not live in our own homes. It can connect us to people we might typically avoid. It can inspire empathy in our hearts. It can encourage us to turn away from reprehensible behaviors. It can help us to laugh at ourselves and at the absurdity of our fears and foibles. It can break our hearts and then help mend them.

All art is about people. Music reminds us we are not alone and our experiences are not unique. Music can challenge our hearts and minds to expand, to critique, to celebrate, and to connect, or it can numb us to pain and send us toward our doom. As an artist, I've seen how music has been a way to explore my fears, frustrations, celebrations, and dreams. It has given voice to my worship. It has drawn me into community. From singing and dancing in my grandparents' living room, to leading worship onstage in front of thousands of people, to entertaining strangers in a pub, to sitting in the backyard with members of our home group listening to someone's latest composition, music has been a constant part of my life. I hope that never changes.

Even if you're not an artist, your faith is a song the world around you hears sung every day. Make it a good song. Let it resonate with the hopes and struggles of your audience. Make it a true song, unafraid to admit to struggle and resolutely pointing toward the light you have found. Make it a beautiful song that paints a picture of the world as God intended it to be and as it will be again. Make your faith a song that others want to sing along with. Make it sensitive to the room, transcendent of your failures, and revelatory of the work being done in you. Find the harmony line and make a chord. Let it twang and rattle and skip beats. Leave room for a drum solo if you want. Then listen to the songs being sung by the others in your tribe. You'll start to recognize a certain rhythm—a consistent cadence—that thrums beneath all of the songs being sung. That's the voice of God calling all of us closer to each other and to himself. That's the heartbeat of transformative community. Music is no accident. It's a beacon. Let it beat true, and learn to dance.

BACK TO THE TWANG

That conversation with Buddy Miller at the pancake house happened just a few months before the new owners began chloroforming True Tunes. In time, I regained my love of music and my ability to sing it. Something was different, though. The songs I wrote were a bit darker, yet laced with a glimmer of hope. I was feeling the tension in those months, but I was living in expectation of a someday-coming resolve.

The twang. It's about unresolved notes bending into resolution, or at least trying to. It's about chaos settling into a groove. It's about pain and fear and sex and loss and a hunger that nothing in this world seems to satiate. The twang is the human condition—bent, rusty, groaning to be made whole. It echoes through generations, from the pages of the Bible to the conversation around our dinner table to the songs I was wringing out of my own guitar. The Stones tapped it when they sang "Satisfaction," but the best music, in my opinion, at least hints at where the resolution can be found. These artists are like sages to me, pointing out which horizon the sun will rise over as the darkness melts. Their twang satisfies me, not with easy answers, but with the fellowship of other travelers and a shared hope. The radical, loving, transcendent, and cryptic words of Jesus reverberate through the ages with the most profound twang of all.

Buddy explained that all great American music is rooted in that twang, but that music factories have surgically removed it — replacing it with smooth strings and synthesizers. Some people (many people, in fact) don't want to be reminded of the tension in their life. They want a soothing escape, a musical bubble bath to take them away. One of the subtle promises of the Industrial Revolution was protection from the twang of life. Machines would make our work easier. Technology would connect us. Might would define and protect "right." Industry would make everything more affordable, accessible, and consistent. The reason modern country wasn't doing it for me, Buddy suggested, was because the twang had been industrially removed and then artificially reintroduced, like when they take all the good stuff out of bread and then "enrich" it with chemical vitamins.

The twang — that essence of vitality and struggle — was suddenly all around me. It was in the black coffee in our cups and the conversation at our table. It was in my favorite art, the best food, the most satisfying drinks, and every relationship that mattered. And everywhere, people were trying to mute it, to resolve it prematurely, or to rebuke it. The twang makes some people uncomfortable, especially people who do not want to admit to the dissonance in their own hearts. Buddy unwittingly prophesied, and I drank it in. For the first time, the tension I had been feeling had a name.

"If that's the music you love," Buddy offered gently, "then you and Michelle should just embrace that twang and see where it takes you."

The taste for twang Buddy encouraged me to pursue provided the courage to embrace what had been planted in my heart decades earlier. In the years since our conversation, it has leaked into all areas of my life. It has affected not only the way I absorb and appreciate art but also how I try to live out my faith. Americana music is authentic by nature, just as farmers markets, house concerts, craft-brewed beer, coffee, and artisanal bread and chocolate should be. And there may be nothing I crave more viscerally than authenticity. In recent years, I've noticed these preindustrial values capturing the attention and affection of hordes of young people and more than a few wizened baby boomers. It's more than just music or chocolate or bread of course, but it definitely echoes through those things in artistic ways that point to a someday-coming resolving chord.

In Ecclesiastes 3, King Solomon reflects on the twang of life. After the famous opening about a time and a season for everything under the sun, Solomon drops this bomb:

> *I have seen the burden God has laid on the human*
> *race. He has made everything beautiful in its time. He*
> *has also set eternity in the human heart; yet no one*
> *can fathom what God has done from beginning to end.*
> *I know that there is nothing better for people than to*

be happy and to do good while they live. That each of them may eat and drink, and find satisfaction in all their toil—this is the gift of God.

ECCLESIASTES 3:10–13

The factory has provided us with lots of stuff but little satisfaction. Never in human history have we been more productive and less at peace. I've watched friends lose interest in their marriages, their jobs, their families, and their faith, trading in the authentic, tested truth for a corporate model that offers convenience and security instead of goodness. I suspect many people walk away from their relationship with God because there isn't enough twang in their community or in their own personal understanding of the heart of God. Or maybe the twang is there, but they never developed a taste for it.

The more processed and polished the Christian experience becomes, the more distant the twang gets. People in pain can't sing along with perfectly resolved, major-key songs for very long. Easy-listening, white-bread theology temporarily washes away people's tension like a warm bubble bath, but it doesn't work forever. The bending notes always return. Instead of trying to avoid or contain the twang, we need to ride it to resolution. For those with ears to hear and tongues to taste, bread, coffee, chocolate, beer, music, gardens, and friendships all resonate with that soulful twang as they point resolutely to the author of all good things.

That conversation with Buddy Miller happened twenty years ago now. Since then, he has become known throughout the world as one of the most respected and celebrated artists and producers in the Americana scene. He's worked with a long list of legends and has released a string of critically acclaimed albums. He deserves every bit of praise that comes his way, but back in 1995, Buddy hadn't released his first real solo record yet. "I don't know if you're going to like it," he said. "It's pretty twangy."

Boy, was it. Thank God.

Chapter 9

SEEKING GOD'S TABLE

ver the last twenty years, through these conversations about bread, chocolate, music, and coffee, it has become increasingly clear that the church—not just our local church but the entire contemporary Western church—has been profoundly more influenced by the values of the Industrial Revolution than she has influenced those values. While I realize there have been resisters all along—and some of them have been quite compelling—those exceptions actually prove the rule. By and large, Christians, individually and collectively, have taken on the values of industrialism and then worked out a gospel that supports those values instead of allowing God's Word to transform us and motivate us to push back against these prevailing principles:

- ◆ convenience
- ◆ conformity
- ◆ expedience
- ◆ comfort
- ◆ entitlement
- ◆ disposability
- ◆ consumerism
- ◆ progress

These are the values of our age. Truth be told, these are the values of brokenness and sin that have plagued us since Adam and Eve chose the convenient, expedient, cheap, comfortable path offered to them by the enemy of everything good, true, and beautiful. But there is no doubt that humankind's ingenuity and industry has brought these values to the forefront of our culture in staggering ways over the last couple of hundred years. It's also no wonder that so many people are ready to be done with it. We have seen technological innovations that none of us could have imagined. Instead of making life substantially better, richer, or more connected, they have left us more isolated and alone than ever. These industrial tools, neutral though they may be in and of themselves, allow us to scratch every itch immediately. So we scratch until we are raw and bleeding. We eat cheap food until we are obese, and yet we are still starving.

It's no wonder that in this day of corporate corruption and the tarnishing of the American Dream, the watching world chooses not to look to the church for answers. The church has developed an accent that renders our words indecipherable to seekers of the good, the true, and the beautiful. We have taken the Enemy's bait again and again, believing that a little more comfort will fill the sanctuary; a little more cash on hand will protect us from a rainy day; and thicker walls will guard us from the evil in the world. The church lost her voice to the culture-at-large when she adopted the values that cheapened our food, devalued human lives, and took the oh so tempting bait of Christendom — those mythological days when Christians supposedly ruled the culture with gospel purity. The gospel is about sacrifice and grace and loving God and our neighbor with our whole heart. Christendom is about human power enforced in the name of God. Whether via Constantine or the Crusades or the Culture Wars, when the people of God trade in gospel living for political power, we, too, often lose the plot. It's no wonder that spiritually minded seekers wouldn't look to organized religion for answers when they see what so much of religion is organized around.

It doesn't take much self-examination to see that I have been complicit in this compromise. I like to feel enlightened—and I may be quick to point to my record collection or home-brewed beer as evidence—but the truth is that these industrial values flow through my heart and mind like the blood in my veins. The challenge is how to respond. As that still, small voice patiently and graciously whispers in my ear that there is a better way, will I hear it and obey, or will I turn up the volume on my headphones and go back to the comfortable world I have created? While I may be justified in my frustration, I allow my pride, irritation, and self-righteousness to keep me from seeing the beautiful examples of intentionally crafted faith and community all around me.

In his goodness, God continues to bake fresh bread— that Bread of Life—and the aroma pulls me in. As I have explored the artisanal revolution, I have smelled it. I have encountered an underground stream of values that motivate and excite many of the practitioners of these new, old ways. Sometimes these values are clearly stated up front. When we see Bill and Chérie Guerrant's farm and taste their food, the underlying values of purity, hard work, and value over cost are all front and center. Sometimes these values are more subtle. Some artisans aren't even consciously aware that they're upholding a value structure. They're just instinctively following their hearts and their hands, trying to do something that feels right. Once we start riffing on these ideas, though, they sing right along.

The hard questions I have to continually ask myself—questions I believe God wants the church to ask as well—are these: As we look at the words and the work of Jesus, would he be more comfortable on one side of this divide or the other? If we say we desire to follow him, then how should that affect how we live, how we love, how we eat? What lessons might be lingering in the aroma of this artisanal reawakening? Can we develop a new, more authentically Christlike accent? I believe we can. I hope I can.

THE ARTISAN JESUS

Jesus was a carpenter (Mark 6:3)—or some kind of construction worker (the Greek word can also refer to a mason or smith). But long before he learned to work with wood, he was an artisan. With his hands, he brought order from chaos. The apostle John opens his account of the life and ministry of Jesus with a fascinating bit of narrative poetry.

> In the beginning was the Word, and the Word was
> with God, and the Word was God. He was with God
> in the beginning. Through him all things were made;
> without him nothing was made that has been made.

> *In him was life, and that life was the light of all*
> *mankind. The light shines in the darkness, and the*
> *darkness has not overcome it.*
>
> JOHN 1:1–5

Modern industrialized religion and polluted, watered-down, self-help pseudospirituality too often miss this. The Word wasn't just from God; the Word *was* God. The Word wasn't part of creation; it *was* the vehicle of creation. The Word is not just bright or one good source of light among many; the Word *is* the light, and it is life. It is so pure and true and good that no darkness can overcome it! The Word isn't a proof text used to support a point; it isn't a political system or a fund-raising mechanism. It is not a step-by-step guide to self-discovery or spiritual superiority. It is a beacon drawing us toward itself. This is amazing stuff. This is the stuff of art.

This Word—*logos* in the Greek—is Jesus. Jesus has been creating things with his hands since the very beginning. In complete and perfect community with the mysterious triune nature of God, together with the Father and the Holy Spirit, Jesus brought light into darkness. God spoke, and Jesus was his Word. Through him, all things were made. All things! I've been scuba diving in sixty feet of water and seen tiny creatures that need not be as elaborately colored or intricately designed as they are. Everything on this planet screams, "Creation!" Jesus crafted the mountains, the seas, the deserts, the animals, the plants, and even human beings according to God's perfectly wise plan. Then he gave us free will and the ability to imagine and dream. He created us "in his image"— a mysterious statement that at least partly points to our ability to be junior creators. We can't speak something out of nothing, but he does invite us to participate in the ordering of our world. He honors our attempts to create. Whether it's bread, coffee, music, a painting, or a community, when we create, we follow in his steps.

In bodily form, Jesus kept on creating. He was a winemaker, a community builder, an architect, a healer, and a storyteller. He was a bread maker and a fishmonger. He drew pictures in the sand that saved a woman's life. His creative power was so intense that the sick were healed with just a thought. He spit in the dust, made some holy mud, and opened a man's eyes.

My favorite creative act of Jesus was gathering blue-collar workmen and marginalized women and crafting them into a force that would change the world. He built a church—and if you've had a bad experience with contemporary churches, I invite you to replace the word *church* with *community*— that subversively sought out, honored, and served the unlovely, the diseased, the broken, and the dead. It breaks my heart to hear people say they love Jesus but have no use for the church. Yes, many of the corporate, industrialized aspects of the modern church bear more resemblance to the local megaplex or department store than they do to a countercultural group of ragged lovers and servants, but deep down, the church is something Jesus established. I believe today he longs to call out to her in her manufactured tomb, like he did to his friend Lazarus, "Come out!"

I have experienced dead church. I have felt queasy whenever harsh, ignorant, attention-starved charlatans make their way onto the TV screen and say all kinds of nonsense in God's name. I've cringed as politicians cheapen the gospel, cherry-picking it for their petty purposes and ignoring the difficult bits. I've railed against hypocrisy, even as I regularly must repent of my own. I've tasted stale, hardened white bread when what I needed was the bread of life. I've sipped the vinegar of bitterness, hatred, and fear when what I needed was the rich wine of salvation. I realize many modern churches get more wrong than right. But when I return to Scripture, I am reminded that when Jesus called me out of my tomb, he placed me in a family he calls church. My deep need for belonging—I believe Jesus put it there as a homing beacon to call me to him.

I've also noticed how deeply ingrained my identity as a consumer is. When I complain about the problems of the church—the manufactured nature, the corporate aftertaste—I do so as a consumer who wants his money back. The more I've worked to see my primary and highest calling in relation to other believers as a servant, the more my capacity for grace and patience has expanded. Jesus invites me to be creative—to speak order into the chaos of community. To be the church by living a life that is deeply committed to other flawed and difficult people. I feel his hands sanding my rough edges and binding me irrevocably to his people. Church is art, or at least it should be. If yours isn't, maybe you should roll up your sleeves before heading for the exit.

After Jesus' resurrection and ascension, the Holy Spirit came to embolden, empower, and galvanize the tiny group of shaky disciples Jesus had left behind. The first chapters of the book of Acts describe the early church as a people transformed. They shared all they had, giving to any in need; they gathered in their homes and in the temple; they ate together, prayed together, and devoted themselves to the teaching of the apostles. I realize this account is descriptive and not necessarily prescriptive, but I don't think it takes much of a theological leap to see that the underlying values were communal, not individual. Truth was proclaimed and argued, and people were fed and healed. Ever the artisan, the Holy Spirit crafted a living, breathing body out of many disparate and damaged parts. In Eden the Father spoke a word and made Adam from the dust and breathed the breath of life into his lungs. In Acts, the Father spoke a word and through his Spirit assembled many different people (members) into one new body, then breathed life into his church. That's art!

LIVING AN ARTISANAL GOSPEL

It's no secret that the Western church is in decline. Many hands have been wrung about the declining church attendance of young adults. It is more and more likely for a person to self-identify as "spiritual" but eschew the tag "religious" or even "Christian." That was the major theme of my youth. I remember a Christian song from the '70s by Scott Wesley Brown called "I'm Not Religious, I Just Love the Lord." Many of the Christian rock pioneers and the counterculture converts of the '60s and '70s equated religion with superstition, ritual, or formality. The cry of the Jesus Movement was for people to embrace a personal relationship with Jesus, not to just go with the religious flow. Many of them had grown up in some type of traditional church that had lost its relevance for them. The modern evangelical strategy, then, was to strip away the trappings of religion — the garments, the Sunday clothes, the liturgy, and even the architecture — and to bring Jesus and his gospel into the streets. Groups of Christians worshiped in tents, on the beach, in coffee shops, in city parks, and anywhere else they felt like it.

I remember floating the idea "I'm not religious; I just love Jesus" with one of the priests at the Episcopal church I grew up in. He had come to visit the youth group one night to answer questions and to share his story. I was probably dressed in my usual fake leather pants and crazy T-shirt, with my hair spiked up as high as it would go. I fancied myself a cultural rebel — a nonconformist — and I nonconformed in all the important rock-and-roll ways. Father Cole, one of the gentlest (and, I now realize, most patient) spiritual leaders I've ever known, lovingly pointed me to James 1:27, where the writer clearly lays out what acceptable religion is, namely, "to look after orphans and widows in their distress and to keep oneself from being polluted by the world."

That shut me up pretty well. Now I cringe inside every time I hear someone say they have no use for religion. It's not that religion itself is bad; it's that we do it wrong. It seems clear that since the temple curtain was torn and God's presence moved out into the world, the practice of religion has changed. The New Testament is riddled with incendiary challenges that take the old sacrificial and ritual system and cast it in a new light. Instead of offering sheep as sacrifices, we are to be living sacrifices, dead to our sin but alive in Christ and moving about the earth as agents of his peace and grace. But like the Israelites of old, we tend to do things our way. It's as if we are telling God, "No, actually, we have a better idea. How about we just gather together periodically, dress up nice, sing some songs, take an offering, and spend the rest of our time reinforcing all of the things we aren't supposed to be doing. While we're at it, let's invest crazy energy screaming in as shrill a voice as possible to the world around us that everyone is going to hell! Yeah, that's it. We'll make sure to enumerate everyone else's sins, to cloister ourselves in a comfy little huddle and be secretly thankful we're not like those people. We'll answer complicated questions with simplistic answers and give what we can to the poor after we've satisfied all our own wants."

Jesus said a watching world will know we are his people by the love we show for each other (John 13:35), a love that is serving, self-sacrificial, risky, and vulnerable. By and large, though, the world seems to recognize Christians by our obnoxious behavior. It's no wonder so many people say, "No thanks." And while there is definitely something to be said for making faith accessible, by bending over backward to make the gospel relevant, I fear we have cheapened it and turned it into just another product for the culture to consume or reject.

The Industrial Revolution and the values of technocracy and consumerism have shaped the practice of Christianity over the last five hundred years far more than the words Jesus spoke. Our gospel has become a product, and too many of our churches have become no more than distribution points for that product. The gospel I experienced during the charismatic and evangelical era of my upbringing was all about emotional experiences and sin management. Sin was the problem, and the gospel (Jesus' death and resurrection) was the solution. Euphoria was the side effect. Like a convenient tool, all of the mystery and wonder and beauty of the gospel was reduced to something I could pull out when I needed to fix something or someone.

The result of all of this automation and itch scratching is a religion that bears more of a genetic resemblance to a self-help seminar at a Walmart than it does to the words, the work, and the person of Jesus. In fact, I think many people who reject Christianity have never even had a chance to reject Jesus himself. They have been turned off by the political, pharisaical, industrial premise of modern Christianity before being given the chance to experience the loving, generous, grace-filled Savior beneath. We speak of the things of God with such a corporate accent that the world can't even understand what we are saying.

Jesus didn't conform to the world; he transformed it and then demanded we do the same. Although the spread of the gospel was aided by technologies of the day (Roman roads and written language, for instance), Jesus never seemed as interested in setting up systems as he was in sparking community. He communicated deep truths in stories and sought out the weak, the marginalized, the sick, and the broken. He empowered fishermen and other craftsmen to carry on his work instead of recruiting the religious or political elite. He revealed his glory and pointed to the next world by performing miracles in this one. He saw straight into people's hearts and spoke directly to their needs—whether or not it was what they wanted to hear.

Jesus didn't just allow anyone to make up whatever they wanted in his name. In his most famous sermon, he outlined his purpose and outlawed the type of individualistic, relativistic faith crafting that postmodernism celebrates. "For truly I tell you," he preached on the mount, "until heaven and earth disappear, not the smallest letter, not the least stroke of a pen, will by any means disappear from the Law until everything is accomplished" (Matthew 5:18). He didn't come to abolish the law, but to fulfill it in a way we never could. He offered life, but only after death. His wasn't a cheap offer. It cost him dearly. And he knew his followers would be rejected by the world—he wasn't naive. But when Christ followers are rejected by the world, it should be because the type of counterintuitive behavior we display is a stumbling block to the victimizers and the powerful, not because we are selfish, materialistic, angry, or judgmental. We are told God's kindness is intended to lead people to repentance (Romans 2:4). It's difficult to be kind to people while you are yelling at them.

Jesus' words are difficult. They are scandalous; they are subversive; they are exclusive. He uses language the way a master builder uses carving tools and cornerstones. His words are poetic, specific, mystical, and practical—all at the same time. From the highest palace dweller to the lowest street beggar, and from the rich young ruler to the woman at the well, he offers life—a life to be experienced "to the full" (John 10:10). He began the process of healing his entire creation from the ravages of sin and fear and death. He even allowed himself to be swallowed by the grave so he could defeat death from the inside out.

And we have turned him into a candy bar in a vending machine.

We act as if Jesus just wants to be an accessory in our life, like our favorite T-shirt. We put him on, talk about what we believe, and then go back to the feeding trough of false religion and idolatry. He called himself the Bread of Life and said his body is good food and his blood is good drink. We nod and choke down Twinkies.

Jesus invites us to lay down our lives, our securities, our hopes, and our dreams so he can heal them and give them back to us fresh and new. He places us in community with people who are loudmouths, failures, frauds, and crooks, just like we are. He invites us to raise the dead and to walk on the water in the midst of life's storms. And we turn him into a robed guru dispensing platitudes designed to make us feel better about ourselves.

Jesus is the ultimate craftsman. He turned the confession of a flawed follower into the rock on which he would build a church so powerful that the gates of Hades had no power to defeat it (Matthew 16:18). He ate and drank and laughed and teased. He partied with tax collectors and ne'er-do-wells and had dinner with Pharisees like me. But he always told it like it was.

So again, this journey into a sort of premodern, handcrafted, artisanal world feels much more closely connected to the ministry of Jesus than the hyped-up, highly processed, industrialized church culture I see fading around me. I am reminded that the Christian experience is essentially communal. Even the Trinitarian nature of God speaks of community. I am my brother's keeper. I am called to place the needs of others above my own and to serve others. At the Last Supper, Jesus showed us exactly what that meant when he washed his disciples' feet.

God invites us to participate in the creative process with him and within his loving boundaries. When we stray, he promises to find us and bring us back. Finding the boundaries requires discernment — one of the most critical skills a disciple can cultivate. I am convinced it's worth the effort to cultivate tasting skills that will allow me to notice and appreciate the subtle flavors of life and to recognize hidden beauty. Redeeming my palate from the abuse I have inflicted on it is a way of honoring God's creation and of renewing my mind. Oh, that I could completely lose my taste for the fake stuff. Like a recovering addict, though, the potential for failure remains. All I can do is put one foot in front of the other and walk on the water.

Bread, chocolate, coffee, beer, music — it's all just stuff. As much as I believe God made all things good, and as thrilling as it is to pick up a whiff of the eternal in an unlikely place, heaven help me if I confuse these gifts with the giver. I'm sure at least some of the Israelites justified the golden calf by saying that God made both gold and calves, so really the idol should ultimately direct everyone's attention to him. I hope I'm not overspiritualizing again. I do that, you know.

In confirmation class, I learned that a sacrament is "an outward and visible sign of an inward and spiritual grace." Therefore, cultivating a taste for the good, the true, and the beautiful is a sacramental process. How amazing is that? There are outward and visible signs everywhere around us. They are just waiting to be cultivated, tasted, smelled, seen, heard, and touched. I hope we can cultivate a taste for them so we don't miss the "inward and spiritual grace" part. I suspect if more people were inspired to cultivate an artisanal faith — one committed to community, purity, and discernment — more of the world would sing along.

So here's to good food and good drink. Here's to the master of the party. Here's to grace and peace. Here's to mercy when we stumble and fail. Here's to the songs that melt our hearts. May the Lord, the author of life and the architect of beauty, fill our souls with a hunger that nothing in this world can quite satisfy, so we will always seek his table and nothing less.

HELP SOMEONE LESS FORTUNATE CRAFT THEIR OWN STORY

I'm fortunate to be able to speak at colleges, festivals, conferences, and churches from time to time. People often ask me for specific examples of things they can do right away that will put hands and feet to their faith and maybe help them break free of the narcissistic rut their corporate Christianity has left them in. This is an easy question to answer.

When I was a teenager, I went to a concert where an amazing guitarist, songwriter, and singer named Phil Keaggy performed. All he needed was an acoustic guitar and a microphone to hold a thousand people captive for an entire evening. Halfway through his concert, he talked about a specific way each of us could change the life of a child facing life-threatening poverty. He described the Third World poverty he had seen firsthand. With the sensitivity and artistry of a songwriter, he propelled the faces of vulnerable, precious children into our hearts. His passion for justice only added to his impact. That night, Phil Keaggy added something tangible to his otherworldly art as he connected the craft of song to the mission given by Jesus.

The idea of intervening in another person's story in such a powerful way seemed fantastically subversive to a punk like me. When I was about ten years old, I was moved by a Jerry Lewis telethon to go door-to-door collecting donations for muscular dystrophy. I think I scraped thirty-seven dollars together and happily sent it off. I felt good, but the feeling faded, and I never knew whether or not the money had any impact. The chance to help one person — a real person with a name and a face and a story — now, that was a different story. So I gathered my friends together at youth group, and we sponsored a child through Compassion International.

I've been a fan of Compassion ever since. I've seen their long-haul commitment to financial integrity, holistic love, and community empowerment. I've met adults who had been sponsored as children and had dedicated their lives to paying that gift forward. I've seen the fruit of lives transformed by others' generosity and care. In 2007, Compassion invited my wife and me to come to Ecuador to see their work in person. To call it a life-changing experience would be an understatement.

If you've never responded to the opportunity to partner with Compassion, I beg you to do so right now. Compassion partners with local churches to create sustainable programs that offer an education, nutritional meals, mentoring, and spiritual care for more than one million children around the world. Because of my personal experience, you can trust me when I say I've never seen a more cost-effective way of changing the world.

High on a mountain outside of Quito, we hiked to a small "house" that was home to one of the families served by Compassion. The sponsored child, then a teenager, pulled out a box of letters from his sponsors in America. He told us about how much their love encouraged him. This young man would soon be heading to college, where he planned to study environmental science so he could get a job protecting the very mountain he called home. This young man was full of world-shaking excitement. I have no doubt he did everything he said he would—all because one family concluded that thirty dollars per month was a small price to pay for a changed life.

I've met the local Compassion partners—pastors and teachers from the area who do amazing things with resources far less than most of us spend on coffee or beer in a month. Some of them are even affiliated with sustainable fair-trade coffee or cacao plantations. Follow me on Twitter (@JohnJThompson) for updates as we explore ways to profoundly impact people through Compassion's ministry.

I cherish the letters and crayon drawings we receive regularly from our sponsored child, Zulmy, in Guatemala. I hope to visit her someday. Because Zulmy is so well cared for by Compassion, she has no reason to make the terrible journey that so many children are making as they flee violence in Central America to try to find refuge in the United States.

A few years ago at the Cornerstone Festival, I had the honor to present the Compassion opportunity to the crowd. Headlining that night was none other than Phil Keaggy. He offered to play instrumental music as I shared about our experience in Ecuador, and then he played a song he had written for Compassion. The next day, a friend told me he had known about this ministry for decades but had never sponsored a child. That night, he and his daughter picked up a packet and saw the face of a little girl they knew God was calling them to help. "Thanks," he told me. I got chills.

Please consider sponsoring a child today. Then make sure to write to your child and tell them you are praying for them. If you think you can't afford it, I challenge you to evaluate how much you spend on coffee, meals at restaurants, cable TV, and Internet services. You could be saving a life from sex trafficking, disease, violence, or starvation. And even more satisfying, the care your sponsored child receives will shape his or her understanding of the gospel. In places torn by religious strife, superstition, fear, and corruption, Compassion programs introduce kids and their families to the true God, the one who loves them and wants to know them. The reward as you see this child grow is like nothing else. I promise you it will be some of the best money you will have ever invested.

For more information, visit www.Compassion.com/JJT and look around. If you have questions or concerns, contact me through my blog at www.JohnJThompson.com and write "Compassion" in the subject line. I will do my best to respond to you personally. Do it now. Someone is waiting. I can't wait to hear the story of how his or her life was changed because you stepped up and said no to poverty in the name of the good, the true, and the beautiful.

ACKNOWLEDGMENTS

*L*ike bread, chocolate, coffee, or a good craft beer, this book would never have come to be without the mentors, experts, supporters, challengers, and coaches who have spoken into my life, cultivated my tastes, and shown me where the good ingredients could be found.

Thank you, Lord, the author of truth and the creator of beauty, for leaving so many tantalizing clues that point to your goodness and love for us. Thank you for the blessing of community, friendship, and creativity. Thank you for your grace and mercy as we stumble toward you. If any good comes from this book, it is to be attributed to your goodness and mercy. For all of the shortcomings and mistakes, I take full blame.

My wife, Michelle, has always been my favorite sounding board, best friend, cocreator, and champion, and our kids are simply the coolest offspring any parent could hope for. Jordan's coffee prowess and love of nature inspire me. Wesley's cooking chops and quirky humor make me proud. Trinity's artistry and her passion for people and friends remind me that this life is all about community. Jesse's creativity and energy keep me young. There have been strange twists and turns on this road we've traveled together, and I thank God I get to experience it with you five miracles.

To my parents, Tom and Barbara Thompson — you continue to encourage and inspire me in many ways, and for that, I am so thankful. To my grandparents, aunts and uncles, brothers, sisters-in-law, cousins, and grafted-in family members from around the world — thank you for providing the kind of springboard that makes a person feel like he can fly. To Leonard and Judy Thomason (my mother- and father-in-law), and the rest of the Thomason side of the family — your love and support are so much appreciated. A special word of gratitude to my cousin Kennon for our conversations on the streets and beaches of the California coast that convinced me these ideas were worth exploring in greater depth.

To Randy Schoof, Mike Cochrane, Dave Miller, and our Warehouse Church family — thank you for shaping me and giving me a spiritual home. To Jim and Kim Thomas and our Village Chapel family in Nashville, and to all of the members of our amazing home group — I'm grateful for you. The faces and hearts that fill our home — along with their increasingly large number of little ones — constantly remind us of why we moved to Nashville in the first place.

To all of the pastors, mentors, youth pastors, priests, counselors, and teachers who have shaped me, taught me, and tolerated me — I owe all of you a debt of gratitude. To David Bunker, a hero and mentor — thank you for honoring me with your wisdom, advice, and encouragement since I was a teenager. And to Glenn Kaiser and my Cornerstone Festival family—thank you for inspiring me in so many ways.

I'm deeply grateful to Joel Miller for providing the initial championing of this book; to my editor, Carolyn McCready, for your enthusiasm and patience; to Ramona Garnes, my personal writing coach and teacher for more than twenty years; and to Andy Meisenheimer for helping me wrestle this beast to the ground.

A hearty toast is raised to my good friends and fellow writers Doug Van Pelt, Bruce Brown, Lori Heiselman, and Jeff Elbel. And much gratitude goes out to Bob DeMoss, Mark Maxwell, Chris Hauser, Jeffrey Kotthoff, Jeremy Gudauskas, Esther Fedorkevich, Ryan Richardson, and George Barna for your encouragement and support.

To Eddie DeGarmo and Casey McGinty, as well as the rest of my Capitol CMG family and all of my music industry friends in Nashville and beyond—thank you for encouraging me and challenging me both professionally and personally.

To Nate Ernsberger, Mark Hollingsworth, and the rest of the Compassion International team—thank you for entrusting me with your message and for continuing to release children from poverty in Jesus' name. Thank you for taking such good care of little Zulmy in Guatemala and for providing hope and practical help for all of the children in your charge. You are the real deal, and I pray you can reach another million children in the coming years. I'm sure you will.

To the old True Tunes community — staff, bands, readers, friends, and fans — I'm counting on you to help me reconnect with as many of our people as possible. To the artists who continue to craft amazing music despite lingering obscurity and ongoing struggle — thank you for all you do and for your creativity and perseverance. If any readers of this book are open to having their minds blown by talented artists who truly "do it for love," please visit my blog, follow me on Twitter, or subscribe to my online playlists. I can provide a sound track to listen to as you read this book.

Deepest thanks go out to the people whose insights have enriched this book. This includes but is not limited to John Jasiak, Buddy Miller, Scott Witherow, Steve Dresselhaus, George Howell, Bill Cross, Randy Kerkman, Don and Dave Sergio, Carl Meier, Nick Purdy, Bill Guerrant, Chris Barber, Uncle Jerry, Grandpa Holton, my friend in the music business "Anonymous" Wayne, Rob Anstee, Chris Lagrassa, Tommy Ogle (we miss you!), and Dan Knowles. Although I didn't talk to them as I wrote this book, thanks to Wendell Berry for speaking to my heart through books and essays and to N. T. Wright for expanding my understanding of the gospel.

I'd love to hear from you and to continue this discussion in the months and years to come. Follow me on Twitter (@JohnJThompson) and subscribe to my blog at www. JohnJThompson.com to keep in touch.

INFORMATION AND CREDITS FOR CHAPTER TITLE PAGES

Introduction: My antique May Bell banjo uke, crafted by Slingerland in Chicago sometime in the 1920s. I dug it out of a church rummage sale at St. Mark's Episcopal Church in 1988, and my buddy Tommy Ogle fixed it up just a few years ago. Photo by John J. Thompson.

Chapter 1: Yours truly, circa 1973, age three, already in love with records but not yet aware of how to properly hold them. Photo by my aunt, Nadia Jaques.

Chapter 2: I came across this hand-hewn bench along a trail in Ireland in April 2014. I had no idea how old it was, but it had been there awhile and had no problem supporting me when I needed a rest. Photo by John J. Thompson.

Chapter 3: Desem whole wheat rustic bread from Bella Nashville Bakery. They mill the whole grain flour every day right in the shop and bake it fresh. It's chewy, complex, and satisfying. Photo by John J. Thompson.

Chapter 4: Cacao beans, freshly received by Olive & Sinclair and ready to be turned into some of the best chocolate in the world. Photo by John J. Thompson.

Chapter 5: A batch of Ethiopian Yirgacheffe coffee cooling after being perfectly roasted at Nashville's Bongo Java Roasting Company. Photo by John J. Thompson.

 Chapter 6: A glass of The Black Abbey's Wicket Gate American stout served onsite at the brewery's Fellowship Hall in Nashville. The name recalls the beginning of Christian's journey to the Celestial City in John Bunyan's *The Pilgrim's Progress*, which itself was inspired by Matthew 7:13–14. Photo by John J. Thompson.

 Chapter 7: My youngest son, Jesse, planted this carrot in late spring. Although he harvested and ate the other carrots he had planted, he let this one grow and grow and grow. Photo by John J. Thompson.

 *Chapter 8:* Michelle and I traveled across Ireland with musician and teacher Michael Card and a fantastic group of friends in April 2014. This performance at Holy Trinity Church, Crom, ranks as one of the highlights of my life. Photo by one of our friends on the trip.

 Chapter 9: Our dining room table during a wonderful evening with friends, family, chicken mole enchiladas, and lots of laughter. Photo, and enchiladas, by John J. Thompson.

Postscript: This photo was taken by one of our home-group members, Tyler Malone (about. me/rtmalone), when he traveled with a group from our church to serve with the Village of Hope ministry in Uganda. Tyler is a multimedia engineer and photographer living near our home in East Nashville. All of the kids at our church made personalized greetings to send to the kids in Africa. The little kid with the messy hair in the photo inset is my son, Jesse Thompson. Village of Hope, like Compassion International, is a fantastic, life-changing ministry. (villageofhopeuganda.com)

Acknowledgments: A group of guys from our home group went backpacking, and we found ourselves on the ridge of a mountain littered with naturally occurring flat stones. We spent a few hours gathering these stones, placed them into a carefully organized pile, and topped it with one massive flat stone that must have weighed at least a couple hundred pounds. This "table in the wilderness" served us well while we camped there, and I hope it's still standing as a monument to the power of community and friendship. Photo by John J. Thompson.

Information and Credits for Chapter Title Pages: Photo of the Nashville Farmers Market by John J. Thompson.